Studying Cha

Approaching the Canterbury

Studymates

25 Key Topics in Business Studies
25 Key Topics in Human Resources
25 Key Topics in Marketing
Accident & Emergency Nursing
Business Organisation
Constitutional & Administrative Law
Cultural Studies
English Legal System
European Reformation
GCSE Chemistry
GCSE English
GCSE History: Schools History Project
GCSE Maths
GCSE Sciences
Genetics
Geology for Civil Engineers
Hitler & Nazi Germany
Land Law
Law of Evidence
Memory
Organic Chemistry
Practical Drama & Theatre Arts
Revolutionary Conflicts
Social Anthropology
Social Statistics
Speaking Better French
Speaking English
Studying Chaucer
Studying History
Studying Literature
Studying Poetry
Studying Psychology
Understanding Maths
Using Information Technology

Many other titles in preparation

Studying Chaucer

Approaching the Canterbury Tales

Gail Ashton

BEd(Hons) MA PhD

www.studymates.co.uk

© Copyright 2000 by Gail Ashton

First published in 2000 by Studymates, a Division of International Briefings Ltd, Plymbridge House, Estover Road, Plymouth PL6 7PY, United Kingdom.

Telephone: (01752) 202301
Fax: (01752) 202333
Editorial Email: editorial@studymates.co.uk
Customer Services Email: cservs@plymbridge.com
Series web site: http://www.studymates.co.uk

All rights reserved. No part of this work may be reproduced or stored in an information retrieval system without the express permission of the Publishers given in writing.

Gail Ashton has asserted her moral rights to be identified as author of this work.

Printed and bound by The Cromwell Press Ltd, Trowbridge, Wiltshire.
Typeset by PDQ Typesetting, Newcastle-under-Lyme, Staffordshire.

Contents

Preface	**9**
Introduction	**11**
Tackling the text	11
Chaucer's life	12
Chaucer's literary output	14

Part One: Voice and speaker – who tells the tale?

1	**The role of the host**	**16**
	One-minute summary	16
	Introducing the poem	16
	Inconsistencies and problems	17
	Taking charge	18
	Quarrelling and quiting	19
	The Host as man	20
	Harry versus the pardoner	20
	Authority and control	22
	Reading and manliness	22
	The authority to judge	23
	Tutorial	24
2	**The anonymous 'I'**	**26**
	One-minute summary	26
	What is he like?	26
	Observer and chronicler	27
	Who am I?	27
	A straight reading?	28
	Chaucer-the-pilgrim	29
	Which Chaucer speaks?	29
	Shaping a narrative	30
	Reading and interpretation	31
	Tutorial	32

3 Multiple voices: The other 'I' — 34

One-minute summary — 34
Idealising Griselda — 34
Manipulating the audience — 36
The intention of the tale? — 37
Other possibilities — 38
Fracturing authority — 38
Conclusion — 39
Review of section — 39
Tutorial — 40

Part Two: Story and genre – what sort of tale?

4 Genre and story — 42

One-minute summary — 42
Story and analogue — 42
A hybrid form — 43
Playing with genre — 44
Patterns and expectations — 45
Storytelling — 46
Distilling the form — 47
Juxtaposition and contrast — 49
Opening up to question — 50
Creating a gap — 50
Tutorial — 52

5 Speaker and story — 54

One-minute summary — 54
Allocating the tale — 54
Setting up the story — 55
Matching the tale — 57
Review of section — 59
Tutorial — 59

Part Three: A thematic approach – the presentation of women

6 Exemplary and idealised women — 61

- One-minute summary — 61
- The ideal — 61
- Inner and outer virtue — 62
- Speech and silence, moderation and meekness — 64
- Framing and idealising — 66
- Clarifying it — 68
- Tutorial — 69

7 Subverting the ideal — 71

- One-minute summary — 71
- Raising questions — 71
- Meaningful silences — 72
- Subversive speech — 73
- Shattering the ideal — 74
- Autonomous action — 76
- Weaknesses in narrative voice — 77
- Other possibilities — 78
- Compounding the question — 80
- Review of section — 81
- Tutorial — 82

Part Four: Writing and authority

8 Knowledge and experience — 84

- One-minute summary — 84
- Institutionalising authority — 84
- Authorising marriage — 86
- Everyday experience — 87
- A struggle for power — 90
- A material evidence — 91
- Tutorial — 92

9 Fracturing authority — 94

- One-minute summary — 94
- Raising possibilities — 94
- Personal interpretation — 95
- The authority debate — 97
- Debunking the myth — 99
- Subverting and rejecting — 101
- Care of the soul? — 102
- A perfect exchange — 103
- Eliding closure — 104
- Conclusion — 106
- Review of section — 107
- Tutorial — 107

Wider reading — 109

Web sites on Chaucer — 111

Index — 117

Preface

Written some six hundred years ago by Geoffrey Chaucer, *The Canterbury Tales* is a lengthy but incomplete miscellany of individual poems, each related by a different narrator. The stories exist as part of a fictional storytelling contest designed to pass the time for a group of pilgrims on their way to Canterbury. Yet, this dramatic framework binds the tales only loosely, at times receding or even disappearing altogether. The structure of this collection of apparently disparate narratives is, then, a complex and shifting one.

A host of fictional voices and a kaleidoscopic array of stories fight for domination: saint's life, epic, romance, beast fable, sermon, fairy tale or *fabliau*. Some are comic, others serious. Some are greatly affected by the agenda and interjections of their fictional narrators, others not at all.

Questions rapidly accumulate: What is the relationship between individual poems, between tale and teller, between speaker and author? How are we to read the *Tales*? As a collection where all is intertextual or each narrative as a stand-alone text? What is the role of the 'I' who observes and relates the entire poem ? Or of Harry Bailly, the Host of the storytelling drama? To whom do the stories belong and whose viewpoint are we to believe?

So, themes and ideas concur, clash, and compound each other, each resisting appropriation or final definition. Instead, *The Canterbury Tales* heaps multiplication upon multiplication to slide away from us into openness and ambiguity. In this way, as we shall see, Chaucer confronts the purpose and very nature of writing itself.

The aim of this short, critical study is to introduce you to some of the features of Chaucer's most well-known work. It begins by placing Chaucer in his medieval context before identifying levels of narration and some of the possibilities raised by the notion of fictional voice. Further study moves towards a focus upon narrative art by exploring Chaucer's use of genre and speaker. Later sections examine some of this author's main interests – love, marriage, knowledge and experience, religion – by analysing the ways in which he off-sets institutionalised ideals against the practice of ordinary life.

This, plus a range of interactive material, will guide and support you in your studies, whatever your level of expertise. Chaucer's work is questioning, open and, at times, potentially subversive. It fractures authority and shatters long-held ideas. Similarly, this book is intended to provoke thought, to stimulate discussion and sharpen your critical faculties so that you can make up your own mind about this fascinating and complex text.

Gail Ashton

gailashton@studymates.co.uk

Introduction

Tackling the text

It is important to remember that during Chaucer's time English was not as standard or as commonly used as it is now. It existed as a range of regional dialects, of course, and was sometimes used in written texts. For official or serious documents, however, Latin was the norm. The most prestigious tongue was Norman French, especially in royal circles.

Though Chaucer was not the only writer of his time to write in the vernacular (English), he was probably one of the first to make deliberate and consistent use of it, demonstrating its flexibility and offering it as a serious challenge to French and Latin.

At first sight Middle English can appear daunting, but it is actually much easier than you think. Always buy the best edition you can afford. As well as summaries of the tales, such publications also have a same-page vocabulary list where difficult constructions or exceptional meanings are given. Use this list *first* and the glossary at the back of most books only when in grave doubt. Try not to learn Middle English like a foreign language but, instead, use the following tips to help you begin. Be patient. It may take some time to get used to and your reading of it will probably lack speed.

1. Most words are similar to our own but will have been pronounced in the French style with the stress on later syllables or the final 'e' (like French songs) as in 'fressh*e*' or 'smal*e*'. If you 'say' it as you read, and modernise it, you will recognise most of the words. For example, 'dore' will be 'door', 'fals' will be 'false' and 'shewe' 'show'.

2. Occasionally a word has several meanings (like 'corage' meaning 'courage' but also 'heart' or 'sexual desire') or else

has shifted over time ('daungerous' is not 'dangerous' as you might expect but 'aloof' or 'stand-offish'). Some have no modern equivalent ('gentillesse' is stronger than 'gentility'). Use your edition's vocabulary list to help you here.

3. There was no consistent spelling system so that the letter 'y', for example, might represent our 'g' [yaf- gave] or 'i' [lif or lyf – life].

4. Notice tags and filler words like 'eek' [also], 'whilom' [once], or 'sikerly' [truly]. These are soon picked up, but if you are in doubt make a short vocabulary list to keep alongside your text.

5. Watch out for words derived from French like 'daunce' [dance], 'flour' [flower], 'remembraunce' [remembrance], or 'curteisye' [courtesy].

6. Re-arranging word order into more familiar form may help. For example, 'To chirche was myn housbonde borne' becomes 'My husband was carried to church'.

7. Notice peculiar verb forms like 'maken' [to make] or 'maden' [made], or an extra 'y' at the start to denote the past tense as in 'yboght' [bought].

8. You may find a run of negatives ['ne', 'nevere', 'nat', 'noghte'] in the same construction. The meaning is still negative. The number simply strengthens the effect.

Chaucer's life

What do we know of Chaucer's life? Manuscript evidence and surviving official documents reveal that he was a soldier, a civil servant, an ambassador and a court poet, a man with close ties to no less than three royal households. He appears to have been well-travelled and a loyal, circumspect retainer despite the political upheaval of his time.

Introduction

1340–44c.	Born into a well-to-do family of London wine merchants.
1357c.	Entered household of Countess of Ulster as retainer, probably a page.
	Accompanied Prince Lionel on French military campaign.
1359/60	Records show king ransomed him after capture by French.
	Paid as ambassador/envoy to carry letters home to England.
1360–66	No records extant.
	Married Philippa.
1367	Given safe conduct to travel through Navarre (nature of business for royal family not clear).
1368	Possibly sent to Milan as messenger to Prince Lionel.
1370	Another royal mission, purpose unknown.
1372–3	Sent to Genoa and Florence on king's business.
1374	King Edward grants him gallon pitcher of wine daily.
	Also in receipt of annuities from John of Gaunt.
	Given post of Customs House Controller.
	Took lease on London house.
1375	King Edward granted him lucrative wardship of 2 Kent heirs.
1376	Recorded 'secret business' for the king.
1377	Sent overseas several times on royal business.
1378	Sent to Lombardy on secret business.
1380	Records show cleared of all charges, after intervention of high-ranking officials, of *raptus* (rape or abduction?) of Cecilia Chaumpaigne.
1381	Sent as ambassador to France.
1382	Granted additional controllership of petty customs, imports and exports
1385–6	J.P. for Kent.
1387	Last recorded foreign mission.
	Wife Philippa disappears from records, presumed dead.
1388	MP for Kent.
1389	Appointed Clerk of the King's Works by King

	Richard. Post relinquished 2 years later.
	Took post as sub-forester of royal forest at Petherton Park.
1393	Given gift for loyal service by king.
	Additional annuity from King Richard II, doubled on day crowned.
	Took 5 year lease on house in Westminster.
1398	Richard granted yearly gift of tun of wine.
1398	Henry IV renewed grants and added another life-long one.
1400c	Died.

Chaucer's literary output

Like his contemporaries – Gower, Lydgate, Langland and the anonymous *Pearl-Gawain* poet – Chaucer wrote in the vernacular. Following a medieval tradition of authorship, he adapted earlier oral and written stories and songs/poems from a variety of sources – English, Latin, and French or Italian, for his travels as an envoy would have brought him into contact with the work of poets like Jean de Meun, Petrarch, Boccaccio and Dante.

It is difficult to find evidence of exactly when Chaucer wrote or 'published' his material. In addition, he tended to leave some work incomplete then return later for revision, so the following suggests an order of composition rather than a record of dates.

pre 1372	Fragment A of *The Romaunt of the Rose* (influential French poem).
	Possibly minor poem *ABC*.
	Book of the Duchess (elegy for John of Gaunt's first wife composed between 1386–72).
1372-80	Lyric and minor poems like *The Complaint unto Pity, Complaint to his Lady.*
	What became the tales of the Second Nun and the Monk in *The Canterbury Tales.*
	House of Fame (incomplete, 1378–80).
	Anelida and Arcite (courtly love poem).

1380-87	*The Parliament of Fowls* ('80–82). *Boece* (translation of Boethius's *Consolation of Philosophy*). *Troilus and Criseyde* ('82-86). What became *The Knight's Tale*. Minor poems like *The Complaint Of Venus, Adam Scriveyn*. Series of ballads like *Lak of Stedfasteness, Gentilesse*. *The Legend of Good Women* (ongoing and revised).
1388–92	*General Prologue* and early tales in *The Canterbury Tales*. *A Treatise on the Astrolabe* ('91–92, later additions).
1392–95	Probably most of the *Tales* in the 'marriage' group.
1396–1400	Latest of the *Tales* like *The Canon's Yeoman's, The Nun's Priest's, The Parson's Tale*. Several short poems like *Bukton, Complaint to his Purse*.

1

The Role of the Host

One-minute summary – The figure of the Host constitutes only one level of narration in *The Canterbury Tales*. One feature of Harry Bailly's role is to orchestrate events and speakers in a fictional story-telling contest, a role that places him in control of the dramatic frame (loosely linking the *Tales*) as its judge and overseer. Harry is also *within* that frame where his self-control and control of events is more insecure than we might expect. His voice is filtered through the voice of Chaucer-the-pilgrim. His readings of the tales are often reductive or partial. Harry is representative of masculine authority as a 'manly' man *and* used by Chaucer to undercut that authority. In this chapter we will explore:

▶ introducing the poem
▶ inconsistencies and problems
▶ taking charge
▶ quarrelling and quiting
▶ the Host as man
▶ Harry versus the Pardoner
▶ authority and control
▶ reading and manliness
▶ the authority to judge

Introducing the poem

The *General Prologue* introduces us to a range of characters all gathered at the Tabard Inn in Southwark in preparation for a pilgrimage to Canterbury. We meet a variety of figures, each identified by occupation and/or social rank. We are given careful details of their physical appearance, the clothes they wear or the things that they own, together with an accurate record of their speech. These are our first impressions of those who tell a story in the *Tales*.

But from where – or whom – do these observations come? You may have noticed in the *General Prologue* a speaker identified only as 'I', a member of the company of pilgrims who, before the day is out, has spoken to all of them (I(A), 20–34). This anonymous character informs us of his plan to 'telle yow al the condicioun' of his fellow travellers (38). It is this voice that describes each character in turn, whose sly asides – such as 'I trowe he were a geldyng or a mare' (691) – offer hints to the reader.

In this manner he guides us towards a considered reflection of those involved in the drama of *The Canterbury Tales*. Thus, an important background is established by this so-far unidentified speaker. He records 'th'estaat, th'array, the nombre' (716) of the assembled pilgrims and promises to tell of 'al the remenaunt' of their journey (724).

That same voice also reveals a further feature of this narrative poem when he introduces the Host, Harry Bailly. He tells how Harry sets up a story-telling competition whereby each pilgrim is required to relate two tales, one on the way and one on the return journey. The winner will receive a free supper. The proceedings are overseen by Harry who arranges for the drawing of straws to choose who begins (790–845). He also defines the rules for judgement by calling for stories 'of best sentence [morality] and moost solaas [entertainment]' (798).

So, the stage is set: three layers of narration, three separate sets of speakers, all part of the overall poem.

Inconsistencies and problems

The situation is not so simple, however, for our reading of the entire *Tales* highlights inconsistencies. This huge and ambitious poem is, technically, unfinished. During Chaucer's lifetime it had clearly been revised and reordered, but it remains to us as a selection of fragments. Scholars have put these together in a way that the author might not have necessarily intended.

1. What happens to the first person speaker who sometimes seems to disappear as a presence in the *Tales*?

2. Is it the same voice that speaks in the *Retracciouns* at the end, to apologise for the work?

3. What happens to Harry Bailly, whose interventions and interjections subside so that the dramatic frame is used inconsistently? Later it apparently fractures completely as some characters speak yet have never been introduced in the *General Prologue*.

4. Conversely, other individuals do not tell a story at all, while no-one follows the rules of the contest and tells two.

These are questions you need to keep in mind.

Taking charge

As the instigator of the tale-telling competition Harry Bailly's role is to orchestrate events. It is he who takes charge of the pilgrims and 'by oon assent/We been acorded to his juggement' (817–18).

Harry is able to adopt an appropriate tone with individuals in his efforts to encourage them to tell their stories. His approach to the Prioress, for example, is courteously charming (VII, 445–50), and he gently teases and encourages those who are shy, like the Clerk or the 'I' of the *Tales*. In contrast, his response to the Cook is ribald and jocular. He makes jokes about his stale pies, fly-infested shop, and customer illness caused by hasty preparation or poor ingredients. Yet he reminds him too that he is only joking (I(A), 4346–54).

At the same time, Harry smoothly and efficiently moves on the proceedings. One of his great concerns is to take advantage of time. Twice he urges the Cook 'Now telle on, Roger' (I(A), 4345/4353). Later he demands of everyone 'Now for the love of God and of Seint John/Leseth no tyme, as ferforth as ye may' (II(B^1), 17–19). He shows similar concern at the start of *The Man of Law's Tale*.

Here, he reminds the pilgrims that time wasted is irretrievably lost. He quotes a proverb from Seneca to add weight to his idea, before adding a coarse reference of his own about Malkyn's virginity; once gone, it is lost forever (25–31). The Host reiterates the importance of making haste, and, thus, his own co-ordinating role, with his request at the end to the Parson. He invites him to 'knytte up wel a greet mateere', later begging him to hurry up (X(I), 28/70).

Quarrelling and quiting

A further aspect of Harry's role in the dramatic frame (the contest itself) is his intervention in the quarrels that take place between the other pilgrims. The Friar-Summoner argument interrupts the Wife of Bath and threatens to prevent her telling her story. Harry cries 'Pees!' and later, as the Friar's own tale falters, 'Pees! namoore of/This!' (III(D), 850/1298). He insists that the Friar concentrate on his own narrative and leave the Summoner alone, saying that a man in his position ought to be courteous to all (1286–89).

As well as highlighting Harry's diplomacy and active part in the contest, this interlude also introduces another important notion, that of 'quiting'. The animosity between the Friar and the Summoner is based on intense dislike of each other, *and* of what each represents. Thus, when the Friar laughs at the conclusion of the Wife of Bath's long-winded *Prologue*, the Summoner accuses the Friar of suffering from the same wordiness. He adds that friars are like flies, an interfering nuisance. When the Friar retorts that his story will make us all laugh at summoners, about whom he can reveal much, the exchange degenerates (829–49).

The quarrel resumes after *The Wife's Tale* with the Friar attacking the Summoner as good for nothing, except the dispensation of summonses for fornication. The summoner declares he will 'quite' him at every turn, to expose him as a sham (1280–84/1290–97).

At one level, then, personal rivalry and friction add depth to the dramatic frame. In addition, an argument such as this one – based also on what the other represents – opens up the possibility of debate about crucial issues: here, about the Church and its practices. Equally, at a dramatic level one character tells a tale designed to expose another, to gain personal revenge, to ridicule or 'quite' that person (or tale). Once again, the narration of the *Tales* operates at more than one level.

The Host as man

Harry's interventionist policy does more than reveal the complex workings of the dramatic frame, however. Sometimes his interruptions suggest something about his own character's failings. The observant 'I' of the *General Prologue* describes him as 'myrie', 'Boold of his speche' and the embodiment of manliness (I(A), 755–57). His speech is certainly direct and liberally peppered with oaths. Examples are numerous: 'For Goddes bones!' and 'by Goddes dignitee!' (II(B^1),1166/1169); 'Ey! Goddes mercy!' (IV(E), 2419); 'By corpus bones!' and 'by nayles and by blood!' (VI(C), 314/288). After hearing *The Physician's Tale*, he swears as if mad (VI(C), 287). He sums up *The Shipman's Tale* with 'Wel seyd, by *corpus dominus*' (VII, 435), while, more generally, the Parson asks 'What eyleth the man, so synfully to swere?' (II(B^1), 1171).

The Host's oaths are embedded within his own notion of masculinity. They are declarative and summarise his clear, colourful views. His prosaic and vulgar interruption to *The Tale of Sir Thopas*, the first tale told by the 'I' of the overall poem, humorously judges and dismisses it as worthless. He calls for an end to it, 'For Goddes dignitee!', claiming his 'drasty [rubbish] speche' makes his ears ache and his 'drasty rymyng is nat worth a toord!' (VII, 906/923/950). In particular the coarse and emphatic rejection of the Pardoner's invitation to offer to his relics opens up a potential danger that threatens to destabilise the entire framework of the *Tales*.

Harry versus the Pardoner

The Pardoner's singling out of the Host to lead the way in penance is especially audacious given his previous admission of exactly how he manipulates his gullible audience (VI(C), 412–23). The Pardoner tells how he always chooses one person for public defamation, as an example to others. Here, as part of that charade, he identifies Harry as being the 'moost envoluped in synne' (942), and calls on him to come and offer money to the bag of tricks that he calls his relics.

Without doubt, Harry *is* sinful. The Host of the Tabard Inn and a notorious blasphemer as we have seen, he is guilty of at least two of the sins *The Pardoner's Tale* preaches against. (Possibly the third – gambling – is exemplified by the wager on the contest itself.)

Harry declares his lack of faith in the Pardoner – and in the practice of pardoning itself – by graphically expressing his contempt for the Pardoner's relics. He would, he declares, have him kiss his old excrement-stained breeches and swear it was a saint's relic. Harry wishes that he had the Pardoner's 'coillons' in his hand, and cries 'Lat kutte hem of.../They shul be shryned in an hogges toord!' (952/954–55). When, despite his previous eloquence, the Pardoner refuses to speak and Harry, in turn, will no longer play, it is left to the Knight to smooth over the disagreement (956–68).

This exchange demonstrates how Harry slips out of his role as Host and organiser of the contest and firmly *into* the frame itself. His part in this quarrel reminds us of his dual role, both overseer and participant in the frame. It also momentarily threatens to bring the proceedings to a halt. The fact that Harry takes offence over what is only another of the Pardoner's self-confessed tricks is something to consider more deeply. Harry's chosen terminology is interesting. His reference to the Pardoner's 'coillons', and his command to emasculate him, is especially vindictive given the picture of an effeminate Pardoner depicted in the *General Prologue*. Harry, as mentioned before, is the epitome of masculinity: in stature, in his protective stance towards women and his 'manly' swearing. His outraged resentment appears to stem, in part, from a desire to protect his own status and his 'masculine' image, an image that may not be entirely secure, as we shall see.

Authority and control

This interlude reveals a clash of authority. One such clash is between the Church (via the agency of the Pardoner) and the everyday world represented by the down-to-earth Harry, one where Harry seems to win. However, the question of control is enacted at a far more personal level.

1. On the one hand, the Host's oaths are part of the process whereby he establishes himself as master of the proceedings. His emphatic words seem to ensure that his comments are final or authoritative.

2. On the other, Harry's swearing indicates a loss of self-control. Similarly, his control of the contest is less secure than he imagines as individual speakers 'contradict' his requests.

Harry calls on the Clerk, for example, to tell 'som myrie tale', not a sermon or anything dull in 'high' rhetorical style, but something plain and easy to follow. (IV(E), 9–20). Yet the Clerk offers a serious tale related in elevated, elegant diction. After his comic rejection of *The Tale of Sir Thopas*, Harry insists on a moral, prose tale (933–35). He receives his wish, but in the form of the tedious, wordy *The Tale of Melibee*. Equally, he calls for a 'fable' from the Parson who immediately announces his intention to present a serious sermon instead (X(I), 29/70).

At times, then, the Host's control of events is undercut by the actions of others. Though judge and chair of the contest, he has no real authority over the words spoken by the pilgrims. He is presented as an example of masculinity and masculine authority. Yet simultaneously other aspects undercut that authority, as evidenced by his personal 'failing' and his judgement of the tales.

Reading and manliness

Harry's comments upon his own wife, whom he mentions on more than one occasion, hint at a concealed fear of women. His judgement of two of the richest tales in the collection, *The Man of*

Law's Tale and *The Clerk's Tale*, is brief and dismissive. The first is described as 'a thrifty [worthwhile] tale for the nones [occasion]!' (II(B¹),1165), and the second 'a gentil tale' (IV(E), 1212c). It is the latter, *The Clerk's Tale*, of extreme and impossible perfection in a woman, that Harry thinks his wife should have heard [VI(E), 1212c–e].

The picture of Harry's wife slowly accumulates. The Merchant's bitterly comic tale of an adulterous young wife, offered in revenge for his own marital discord, strikes a chord with Harry. His (partial) understanding of the tale is intimated in the diatribe against deceitful, untrustworthy women that follows it. In fact, as far as Harry is concerned, *The Merchant's Tale* is authoritative proof of women's treachery (IV(E), 2419–26). Briefly, he alludes to a fear of his own wife, 'a labbynge [blabbermouth] shrewe', whose vices he could never fully detail, before abruptly breaking off (2426–40).

We learn more later when he reveals that she encourages him to beat his servants and demands that he avenge her honour with those neighbours who snub her in church (VII, 1897–1907). He is afraid that she will provoke him to lose control of his awesome temper, and that he will murder someone (1913–19). What is clear is that Harry is frightened of his wife: she is 'byg in armes' and he 'dare nat hire withstonde' (1921/1926). Once again he breaks off, but not before he has told how her verbal onslaughts strike at the very heart of the masculinity he represents. She calls him a 'milksop', or a coward 'ape' and says he should exchange his knife for her 'distaf and go spynne!' (1905–12).

Thus Harry's outraged attack on the Pardoner's lack of masculinity is given added resonance. On the one hand, Harry symbolises all that is masculine and authoritative. Yet Chaucer undermines our faith in this representation for Harry is not all that he appears, either in his personal life or as the controlling element of the dramatic frame. Why might Chaucer wish to present him in this way?

The authority to judge

When all agree that Harry can be 'of oure tales juge and

reportour' (I(A), 813), he is invested with authority. The question is, as we have seen, is he up to the job? We have already noted that many of the Host's readings of what he hears are affected by his perception of himself and others. He particularly enjoys *The Nun's Priest's Tale*, a multi-layered narrative that Harry interprets at its simplest and most literal level. He sees it as a tale about the 'marriage' of a potent cockerel whose virility he transposes onto the figure of its teller, the Nun's Priest. Harry praises its telling with 'I-blessed be thy breche [buttock], and every stoon! [testicle]' (VII, 3448), and commends the speaker's own manliness (3451–54).

Here, the art of narration is conflated with masculinity so that story-telling 'becomes' a masculine pursuit. A well-controlled narrative is a well-told tale which is what we all admire. At the same time, Harry's reading of this – and other stories – is a reductive one, a narrow and literal interpretation. Harry reads it as a simple animal fable, which it is, but ignores other important possibilities.

Thus, what the Host offers us is only one way of reading, a closed and 'masculine' viewpoint. In this way Harry's humorous role as interpreter of stories is offered as evidence of a restrictive, masculine authority.

Tutorial

Further reading

1. Read some of the other exchanges that take place as part of the drama of the *Tales*: the *Prologues* of the Canon's Yeoman, the Manciple, the Monk or the Nun's Priest or the quarrel between the Miller and the Reeve.

2. Read, too, Harry's interpretations of some of these tales.

Progress questions

1. How would you describe Harry Bailly's *persona*?

2. Explain the notion of 'quiting' and give some examples.

3. What are the features of the role of the Host?

The Role of the Host

Study tips
1. Skim read the text to begin with rather than work line by line. You will soon discover which sections to re-read in detail by participating in tutorials and familiarising yourself with the work of the critics.

2. Begin by using a modern translation alongside the original and/or read the summary contained in most good editions to give a framework to your reading.

3. Listen to a professional tape and/or use an audio-visual aid to help you with the language.

Revision tips
1. Divide your text into chunks for close reading. Identify key passages to work on.

2. Devise a web that maps out key revision areas. Choose your topics and revise only these.

3. Make a list of key questions and address them.

2

The Anonymous 'I'

One-minute summary – The 'I' of the Tales is both a participant in the dramatic frame *and* a voice outside it, filtering the others. The 'I' acts as a chronicler, a faithful translator but also hints that some readings may be incomplete or reductive. The 'I' identifies himself as Chaucer but is Chaucer-the-pilgrim, a mask. The first person narration is sometimes confusing: who is the 'I' of the *Retracciouns*? How subjective or trustworthy is the 'I' generally? In this chapter we will explore:

- what is he like?
- observer and chronicler
- who am I?
- a straight reading?
- Chaucer-the-pilgrim
- which Chaucer speaks?
- shaping a narrative
- reading and interpretation

What is he like?

Harry's voice cannot be finally authoritative. His comments are filtered through another key speaker, the 'I' who recounts the pilgrimage and the story-telling competition itself. Harry cannot be relied upon to shape 'events' or narratives or to offer an accurate, unbiased commentary upon them. Might we, then, place our trust in this other speaker, the 'I' introduced right at the start?

Like Harry, this 'I' is also a participant in the dramatic frame, another pilgrim on the way to Canterbury. Early on he tells us that he goes out of his way to speak to everyone so 'that I was of hir felaweshipe anon' (I(A), 31–32). He seems a courteous, self-effacing figure, several times apologising for the nature and wording of some of the material he recounts. He begs listeners to excuse his plain speaking, and asks that if he appears offensive 'I prey yow to foryeve it me' (725/743). Equally, he warns us against tales told by those such as the Miller (3167–85), even inviting us to read something else (3181). What he wishes us to understand is that his role is simply that of a reporter who repeats, word for word, what he hears.

Observer and chronicler

One of the effects of a first person narration is to offer an eye-witness account. This the character is able to do because he is part of the pilgrimage and, hence, able to record directly what he sees and hears. It is true that this speaker is an observer, slightly apart from his fellows. In contrast to the Host, we scarcely notice him. His is a near-invisible presence, through which we learn about the *Tales* as a whole. His direct intervention is rare.

The 'I' offers an apparently straightforward chronicle, noting after the Pardoner and Harry quarrel, for example, 'Anon they kiste, and ryden forth hir weye' (VI(C), 968). Similarly, he tells how the Summoner's anger with the Friar causes him to shake like an aspen leaf (III(D), 1665–67). The Friar scowls in return but only speaks directly when the Summoner actually insults him (1265–69). In addition, he relates how the Pardoner interrupts *The Wife of Bath's Prologue* to tell of his one disastrous attempt to marry (III(D), 163–93).

In short, all that we learn of the tales themselves and their speakers through the device of the dramatic frame – even what we know of Harry Bailly – is through the first person narrator. Then who is this speaker? Is his role that of recorder or reporter, as he would have us believe, or something more complex?

Who am I?

This anonymous speaker is eventually identified as 'Chaucer' in links such as 'Bihold the merry words of the Hoost to Chaucer' and

'Here begins Chaucers *Tale of Thopas*', or 'Chaucers *Tale of Melibee*'. The name is apparently confirmed when the 'I' records 'whan ended was my tale of Melibee' (VII, 1889), or how the Host 'stynteth Chaucer of his tale of *Sir Thopas*'.

Our earlier impression of a humble fellow, anxious to avoid giving offence, is confirmed in the exchange between himself and Harry Bailly. When the Host asks 'what man artow?' (695), he is articulating the question on all our lips. Harry notes the man's shyness, commenting on how his eyes are always cast on the ground as if he is searching for a hare. He demands that he approach and 'looke up murily', inviting others to make way for him (696–96). Harry says that he seems 'elvyssh' [preoccupied/ in a dream] (703), and not sociable. He is an enigmatic figure indeed.

When the Host calls for a tale of mirth from him, 'Chaucer' begs that he be not 'yvele apayd' or displeased, for he only knows one tale (706–08). When he is angrily interrupted in mid-story, he is distressed, seeming not to know why he is not allowed to continue as the others have all been; after all, 'it is the best rym I kan?' (928).

A straight reading?

Such humility from what seems to be a rather naive and detached figure could easily be taken at face value. Yet, not only do the tales he recounts demand closer inspection (Read them for yourself and see), but the exchanges that frame them hint at something deeper.

Harry describes this 'Chaucer' as a 'popet', a little doll, and jokes that his waist is as shapely as his own (700–02). In another of Chaucer's poems, *The House of Fame*, there is also a first person narrator apparently called Chaucer. In this tale, he is carried aloft by an eagle that complains about his great weight [*The House of Fame*, 573–77]. Which – if any – of these portraits is actually Chaucer?

Equally, when the 'Chaucer' of the *Tales* hopes that we will like his rhyme, the only one he knows and the best he can do, he is asking us to listen to *Sir Thopas*. We have already noted Harry's dismissal of it as rhyme 'dogerel', one that is plodding and dull (925). This – possibly the worst tale in the collection *if* we are to (mis)read it as serious (as Harry does) – is Chaucer's best? It is followed up by a 'litel' prose story (937), *The Tale of Melibee*, a long, boring morality tale related in a sober, earnest tone.

Chaucer-the-pilgrim

Suddenly this speaker's self-effacing attitude, his acute lack of awareness about the reception of his first tale, seems disingenuous. Are we to take seriously the suggestion that this figure is actually Chaucer, the poet? Or, is the author of the *Tales* having a sly joke at our expense, poking fun at both himself – the great writer – and our expectations of writing and writers? Further evidence that this voice is not the author's is found in the introduction to *The Man of Law's Tale* where the narrator mentions Chaucer by name *without* apparently recognising him in the midst of the pilgrims. The 'I', this fictitious 'Chaucer', records the Man of Law's listing of Chaucer's works (II(B^1), 46–89).

It seems, then, that the 'I' is not Chaucer but the author at one remove, hidden behind a mask or *persona*, speaking through the voice of one named as 'Chaucer' but more usually distinguished by us as Chaucer-the-pilgrim. In this way, the voice that filters all the other voices and stories is itself manipulated and controlled by a hidden author. Thus, an important distinction is made.

Which Chaucer speaks?

In effect, we have identified two Chaucers. One is firmly located in the text as a narrative voice in its own right: Chaucer-the-pilgrim or the 'I'. The other is the author, the concealed controller who writes everything in the *Tales*. Chaucer-the-pilgrim is, then, fictive, an invention of Chaucer-the-author. When he speaks as 'I', however, it is tempting to assume that the views offered are attributable to Chaucer himself (just as it is with all the other speakers). This is, of course, not necessarily the case. The problem is how to tell the difference.

It is a problem compounded by the conclusion to the *Tales*, the *Retracciouns*. Here it is unclear who exactly the speaker is. The voice is first person, but is it Chaucer-the-pilgrim?

Humility and apology mark the writing. The 'I' comments that if the work displeases then attribute it to 'the defaute of myn unkonnynge and nat to my wyl' (X(I),1075–76), and begs Christ to forgive him. Equally, if it pleases, praise Christ and not, by implication, the skill of the author. The speaker is also thoroughly aware of what he has written, listing a variety of poems as evidence (1080–89).

Yet the tone is serious with none of the humour of the exchanges with the Host or the comic parody of *Sir Thopas*. Gone too is the straightforward, observant chronicling of events. This is a moral retraction which revokes all 'translacions and enditynges of worldly vanitees', and begs forgiveness for certain works, such as 'many a lecherous lay' (1083/1078). Other, more erudite and instructive pieces, he commends to Christ and the Virgin Mary, in the hope of salvation (1079–90).

This raises several questions. To what extent is this section *part* of the *Tales*? Is it an afterthought, written by the author towards the end of his career? Is it the voice of someone attempting to put his affairs in order? It is a highly moral conclusion; are we, then, to read the rich tapestry of tales that come before it in the light of this desire for grace, to dismiss the humorous, the vulgar, or the sly asides?

The main focus of our attention here is who speaks. It ends 'compiled by Geffrey Chaucer' for 'Heere taketh the makere of this book his leve.' What remains unclear is whether this is the author, or whether we are still in the dramatic frame of the *Tales* and this is Chaucer-the-pilgrim. What do you think?

Shaping a narrative

Another problem raised by first person narration is that of reliability: to what extent may a voice be trusted?

We saw earlier the way in which Harry Bailly's judgement of tales was prejudiced. Chaucer-the-pilgrim is a faithful recorder of events. From the start he insists upon the importance of accuracy. Whoever does his job, he says, must 'reherce as ny as evere he kan/

Everich a word, if it be in his charge'. Otherwise, he would be narrating 'untrewe', inventing things or using 'newe' [his own] words (I(A), 731–36). His conclusion is that 'wordes moote be cosyn to the dede' (742). So, though it displeases him to retell the Miller's 'cherles tale', he must detail every word, however coarse or offensive, 'Or elles falsen som of my mateere' (3170–75).

His role is, thus, to chronicle or translate. He implies that contrary to what a first person account might suggest, his will be objective; in short, he has no vested interest in what he tells. To what extent do you think he achieves his aim? The predominant feature of the poem centres on this notion of recording, so that 'quod' becomes a key word. He quotes an exchange or an argument within the frame and leaves us to interpret its significance. One such example is the interlude between the Squire and the Franklin, rudely interrupted by the Host whose remarks only gain their full irony in the light of the entire exchange.

In this way Chaucer is able to use the Chaucer-the-pilgrim figure as a means of ordering the dramatic frame, to highlight its interplay. Similarly, by allowing this voice to record several interpretations or meanings of tales (such as Harry's, for example), the intertextuality of the whole is widened.

Reading and interpretation

However, though we are set up for the vulgarity of *The Miller's Tale* which Chaucer-the-pilgrim must objectively report, he also guides us towards *one* interpretation of it. He advises us not to take it too seriously (I(A), 3181). Our enjoyment of the Miller-Reeve quarrel, and the reception of the tales each tells, is heightened. We are also invited to consider more than one meaning of these stories.

Interpreting *The Miller's Tale* as a personal attack, the Reeve 'quites' him with his own story. Yet, Chaucer-the-pilgrim tells us that the others simply laugh at it (3855–58). No-one, except the Reeve, notices any intended slight. Equally, Chaucer-the-pilgrim records that the Cook particularly enjoys *The Reeve's Tale* because he knows a thieving miller (4325–38). The Cook's reading is only one, narrow reading, informed by his own personal animosity towards millers in general. Ironically, it also happens to concur with the Reeve's intention which no-one else has noticed. Thus, alternative readings are presented, none of which is the sole sum of the tale.

So, just as the Host's comments point towards a single reading of a tale, Chaucer-the-pilgrim's 'record' offers alternative, though similarly narrowed, possibilities. In this way, Chaucer is able to off-set voices and to open up interpretation. It is this fracturing of the authority of tales – of finally 'understanding' them in a unified reading – that Chaucer is highlighting when Chaucer-the-pilgrim comments on the nature of authorship just before he tells the story of Melibee.

He notes the way that the four Evangelists tell the story of Christ's life. Each tells, in essence, the same story so that the 'sentence' [meaning/intention] is consistent. But, he asks us to remember that in the telling is 'difference' (VII, 948). Each emphasises, or omits, different features. Thus, though their 'sentence is al oon' (952), their stories differ, just as his 'Melibee' will be his own version (943–61).

Tutorial

Study tips

1. Plan your raids upon the library with friends so that you identify crucial reading material together.

2. Pool your resources so that you share books and articles with others.

3. Be prepared to work collaboratively, swapping notes and each investigating a selected area on behalf of the group.

Revision hints

1. Find your own pattern of working: early on in the day or late at night?

2. Try to revise little and often rather than in large units.

3. Make sure you reward yourself and find time to de-stress.

Discussion points
1. Must we always read Chaucer's work in the light of its original context?

2. How far are Chaucerian texts able to support contemporary theories about literature?

3. How does the presence of a fictional narrator complicate our readings of these poems?

Further reading
Read some portraits offered by this figure in the *General Prologue*: the Pardoner, the Summoner, the Wife of Bath, the Knight, the Prioress, or look at the description of a character like Alison in *The Miller's Tale*. How objective is this voice?

3

Multiple Voices: The Other 'I'

One-minute summary – An individual speaker both directly and indirectly sets the agenda for a tale *and/or* attempts to manipulate its reception. Such a speaker is often not as authoritative as he might think; others read the tale differently, or it is marked by ambiguity or contradiction. Individual narrations vary; all is open and multiple rather than unified as a reading. In this chapter we will explore:

- the idealisation of Griselda
- manipulating the audience
- the intention of the tale
- other possibilities
- fracturing authority
- conclusion
- review of section

The third level of narration is centred on the other voices of the *Tales*. These we hear as individual speakers, such as the Knight, the Miller, or the Reeve. They are additions, not the first person of Chaucer-the-pilgrim but the separate, constantly changing 'I' within what he reports. Thus, each tale is told by a different first person speaker, the strength of whose presence varies from poem to poem. Let us begin by analysing just one of these voices.

Idealising Griselda

The Clerk tells the story of Walter, a marquis both loved and feared by his people (IV(E), 69). Pressured to marry, he chooses a poor peasant girl, Griselda. He then tests her obedience in a series of increasingly bizarre 'assays' [tests].

From the start, the Clerk is not afraid to voice his opinion of

Walter. With his 'I blame hym thus' (78), he delineates Walter's selfishness and focus upon immediate pleasure (78–84). The Clerk chastises him for his initial refusal to wed, a refusal that affects his line and, hence, the entire kingdom. Immediately, we are prepared for the Clerk's favouritism towards Griselda, a bias that marks his narrative. Earlier, the Host described him as 'coy and stille', like a new bride (1–3), a comparison that seems to feminise the Clerk and allies him with the feminine. This is in contrast to what we might expect of this agent of the Church, a moral teacher and scholar, one who represents masculine authority (See I(A), 285–308).

The Clerk's admiration for Griselda and the idealised femininity she symbolises is apparent throughout. It is conveyed through her implied goodness. He lists, at length, the qualities that comprise her 'vertuous beautee' (VI(E), 211–31). He reiterates this when she is finally banished from the palace, calling her 'a flour of wyfly pacience' (919) and, again, detailing her humility and meekness (925–31). In addition, certain key words take on an especial resonance in the workings of a narrative far too complex to explore fully, words such as 'sadnesse', 'pacience', 'contenaunce', or 'corage'.

▶ *Study tip* – Read the tale to see if you can identify a pattern.

The Clerk's extensive praise culminates in the remark, 'Thus Walter lowely – nay, but roially –/Wedded with fortunat honestetee' (421–22).

The Clerk's narration also hints at Griselda's saintliness, with several Christian allusions. Twice, her home is implicitly compared to 'a litel oxes stalle' (207/291). The image is of one lowly born but rich in inner virtue. It is strengthened when the Clerk interrupts noting that despite her birth 'As in a cote or in an oxe-stalle', Griselda is seemingly nurtured in an emperor's palace (394–99).

His narration also orchestrates our response to her by emphasising her vulnerability. The repetition and cumulative effect of words such as 'pitously', 'tendrely', 'yonge', or 'deere' – plus reference to tears and embraces – reach a height in the scene where she is reunited with her children (1080–1106). The effect is one of pathos and is underscored by the Clerk's own summative apostrophe, 'O which a pitous thyng it was to se' (1086). The Clerk wishes us to feel compassion for Griselda's sufferings. In another scene – when the sergeant takes her children, apparently to kill them – he accumulates more religious allusions. He describes how Griselda lulls and kisses her child, marking her with the Cross of Christ (550–60), doing the same when her son is taken later (679–83). The Clerk is calling attention to both a passive patience that he admires *and* the intended lesson of his text (which is about our acceptance of pain, as we shall shortly see). He notes how Griselda offers up her child's soul to Christ, explicitly comparing her innocent daughter's 'death' to Christ's crucifixion (555–60). The scene also suggests that Griselda is likened to the Virgin Mary, while, more generally, she is described as a 'lamb', all meek and innocent and holy (538).

Manipulating the audience

So far the Clerk's colouring of his narrative has been implicit. However, he also intervenes to comment directly upon events and deepen the tale's impact. He cries 'Allas! Hir doghter that she loved so!' (543) before adding that even to a nursemaid – let alone a mother – this 'reuthe' [pity] would be too much to bear (561–63).

This is a blatant attempt to manipulate audience response. His interjections signal open disapproval of Walter's 'wikke usage' (785) in pushing Griselda to 'the outtreste preeve of hir corage' (787). The Clerk notes how previous (unnarrated) tests have only ever 'proved' her loyalty and goodness. What then, he asks, is the point of continuing, even though 'som men' – by implication not himself – 'preise it for a subtil wit?' (459). The Clerk underscores his point with 'But as for me, I seye that yvele it sit' to test needlessly a wife (460). (See also 455–62.)

Apostrophe and exclamation
Later, apostrophe and exclamation intensify the Clerk's distress at Walter's behaviour. He cries 'O nedelees was she tempted in assay!' (621), before going on to remark that married men seem

unable to stop once they find 'a pacient creature' (622–23). In a direct address to women, he asks are these tests not enough? What more proof does a husband want of her 'wyfhod and hir stedefastnesse' (699)?

This appeal to the audience has the dual advantage of highlighting crucial issues and underscoring the tale's emotional impact.

The intention of the tale?

This narrative, then, works through the Clerk himself. It operates both implicitly – in its way of telling, the choice of words and details – *and* explicitly, through his interruptions. Clearly the Clerk has a motive for telling this story. But what is it?

This is the story of Griselda's patient fortitude in the face of suffering. *The Clerk's Tale* ends implausibly happily, with all forgiven. Afterwards, this speaker teaches us its true moral. He says that the lesson of the text is that all humans should accept suffering sent from God, as part of a wider, Christian lesson, especially if a frail woman like Griselda can [1145–51]. Yet, several questions remain.

In telling this story, the Clerk has aligned himself with Griselda and emphasised her as an innocent, saintly victim, passively accepting the 'murder' of her children, yet deserving of our compassion. Does this mean that the narrator is sympathetic to women? His association with the feminine continues when he suggests that few, especially clerks, praise women but that *he* believes no man is as humble or true as a woman (932–38). He indicates that this story is 'inportable' [impossible] as an example of how women ought to behave (1144). Nevertheless, he then adds that women like Griselda are 'rare' these days (1163–69), hinting at an admiration for such implacable inner strength and patience.

Does this tale strike you as one told in defence of women, a question to which we return in a later chapter? Is your response to it one of pity for Griselda? Can you, especially as a modern reader, understand or accept its lesson? Does it raise other more disturbing questions or tensions? There may be a gap between the Clerk's intended effect and the way in which his story is ultimately received.

Other possibilities

The problem of how to read a tale has already been opened up in our exploration of the Host's judgement of the stories he hears. Of this one, he remarked – as we noted earlier – that his wife ought to have heard it.

1. Clearly, his reading is that this is a story of an exemplary woman.

2. Yet, the Clerk himself insists it is impossible for women to attain this ideal.

Immediately, two possibilities are in conflict.

A potential third ending

The situation is compounded by the addition of a potential third ending to this tale. Another 'I' appears, a voice calling itself the Envoy of Chaucer. Who reports its words: the Clerk or Chaucer-the-pilgrim? It further contradicts the Clerk's lesson. The voice seems to speak on behalf of the Wife of Bath and 'al hire secte' (1171), demanding the burial of submissive women like Griselda. It advocates instead female rebellion, a refusal to be silenced or meek and mild, or to allow men – like the Clerk – to tell stories such as this of patient, passive women (1176–1212).

Fracturing authority

The insertion of this voice fractures any notion of masculine authority, in the sense of a unified reading. It returns us to the point raised at the start of this chapter.

1. There, the Clerk as a *persona*, was associated with the feminine, with openness.

2. Equally, as a clerk he is implicated in a masculine tradition of writing and misogyny, as he himself noted in his comment about praising women.

Far from reconciling the two – by writing an authoritative story celebrating women *and* successfully presenting us with a clear moral – the Clerk's narration remains open. His text is marked by ambiguity, tension, and unresolved problems.

Conclusion

Thus, this single example of how an individual narrator attempts to authorise his story also demonstrates what must be the conclusion of this section.

1. A chorus of voices clamour to be heard in *The Canterbury Tales*. Differing speakers struggle to shape and control their narratives, to participate in the dramatic frame under the imperfect control of Harry Bailly.

2. Each direct intervention in their own stories is a significant and, sometimes, ambiguous moment.

3. Each voice, too, is filtered through the so-called accurate 'translation' of Chaucer-the-pilgrim, a comic mask that conceals the author who, of course, manipulates everything.

What remains is not a single definitive version or reading of a tale, let alone of the *Tales* as a whole. Instead, authority is fractured. In its place is multiplicity, openness, and interpretative possibility.

Review of section

In this section we have seen:

1. how *The Canterbury Tales* operates as a collection of individual poems each with its own narrator, yet also within a loosely

constructed dramatic framework, that of the story-telling contest judged and overseen by the Host.

2. three levels of narration and their differing effects:

   (a) the 'I' of Chaucer-the-pilgrim
   (b) an example of an individual narrator
   (c) the Host and his role.

3. the way that this complex narrative method encourages intertextuality (reading between and within the poems), through 'quiting' for example, *and* multiplicity of interpretation.

Tutorial

Further reading
Choose from a selection of very different narratives. See *The Man of Law's Tale*, 'special' voices like the Pardoner, the Canon's Yeoman, the Cook or the Wife of Bath. See too *The Merchant's Tale* or *The Second Nun's Tale*.

Progress questions
1. How does Chaucer layer narrative in the *Tales*?

2. How does the dramatic frame operate?

3. Why so many voices in the *Tales*?

Assignment hints
1. Choose areas of ambiguity or events or moments that are crucial in your text(s). Know them thoroughly.

2. Always quote in the original.

3. Use small phrases or one-word quotes. Choose something suitable for numerous occasions.

Assignments

1. '*The Canterbury Tales* demands to be looked at as a whole; anything less will yield only partial and restricted results. Its meaning cannot be separated from "al that writen is."' (Cooper, 1983). Do you agree with this statement?

2. 'The relationship between teller and tale often comments poignantly on the inadequacies of poetry' (David, 1976). Discuss this comment with reference to at least two tales.

3. What problems are raised by the role and stance of the fictional narrator in any work that you have read?

Research suggestions

1. Remember that Chaucer's *Tales* is the 'record' of an oral narrative, one meant to be read aloud or dramatised. Make/collect your own taped readings or dramatic presentations for some of the poems. *Starting point*: See p. 116, *The Chaucer Studio*, for guidance.

2. Read some other medieval story collections. Discuss the ways in which they operate. Is there a framework? An over-arching theme? A narrator to link narratives or affect our interpretation of them? *Starting points*: John Gower's *Confessio Amantis*; Chaucer's *The Legend of Good Women*; Osbern Bokenham's *Legendys of Hooly Wummen*.

3. Read Chaucer's *Troilus and Criseyde*. Explore the role of the narrator of this poem and his effect upon the story he relates.

4

Genre and Story

One-minute summary – An audience might come to the tale with knowledge of it from other sources, and with an awareness of the patterning of genre. Chaucer disrupts those expectations by manipulating and distorting generic code or a story's analogues. He confronts the limits of generic patterning and the nature of writing itself. Chaucer's opening up of stories and story form multiplies possibilities. In this chapter we will explore:

▶ story and analogue
▶ playing with genre
▶ patterns and expectations
▶ storytelling
▶ opening up to question
▶ creating a gap

Story and analogue

The Canterbury Tales offers us a huge variety of narratives – saint's life, folk tales, romances, epics, fables, dream or love visions, sermons, *fabliaux* or carnival. Some are serious, others bawdy or comic. From where do these stories come?

As we shall see in our final section, the rewriting and retelling of stories was considered entirely normal. Authors participated in a process of 'auctoritee' by taking a previous version or versions and reworking that source. In this way, writing became a web of influences and cross-references. The narrator of the *Tales*, Chaucer-the-pilgrim, highlights this when he confronts the nature of his own narrative. As we already know, he begins by declaring himself a faithful translator of other peoples words and ideas. But, behind him, Chaucer the author presents us with a multitude of stories gathered up into a collection loosely held together by the fictional voices of the Canterbury pilgrims.

Not all of Chaucer's inspiration sprang from fiction. History, philosophy, religious works and treatises, the law and science all influenced his work. We have, for example, the Parson's sermon, the reasoned debate of Melibee and the alchemy of *The Canon's Yeoman's Tale*. Other poems demonstrate a mingling of sources and it is with one of these that our exploration begins.

A hybrid form

The story of Custance's trials in *The Man of Law's Tale* appears to have been well-known in folklore. It conforms to a pattern of motifs found in folk, fairy and romance tales where the heroine is expelled from the parental home and must await rescue and reconciliation with her family. In the meantime she suffers a series of tribulations and tests upon her virtue.

So, Custance is sent to marry the Sultan of Syria escaping with her life on her wedding night. She survives two exiles at sea, a false accusation of murder, and attempted rape before a final reunion and safe reconciliation with her husband and her father.

Folklore is, though, not the only element of her tale. Equally Chaucer's audience would have recognised not only the pattern of her story – itself a part of his chosen genre (romance) – but of other versions of it. Some analogues of this tale have an alternative motivation for her initial journey to Syria. Chaucer and his contemporary Gower, who includes the poem in his *Confessio Amantis*, have marriage as its impetus. Yet another work of the same period, Thomas le Chestre's *Emaré*, adopts the more usual telling of her story recording how she is cast adrift in a rudderless boat after refusing her father's incestuous advances.

Though each might be categorised as romance, each too offers a different emphasis and interpretation of events. From our point of view an immediate question is raised when Chaucer not only omits the 'typical' incest element of Custance's tale but then permits his fictional narrator implicitly to draw attention to it. The Man of Law declares he will speak only of good women and not of those like the wicked – and incestuous – Canace $(II(B^1),77–89)$.

Here Chaucer plays upon the audience's anticipation of events. It already knows how a particular genre (in this case romance) operates. If, in addition, it is aware of alternatives to the same story then a complex set of expectations inform the tale's reception.

As a romance is, however, only one way of interpreting *The Man of Law's Tale*. Another analogue is Nicholas Trivet's *Anglo-Norman Chronicle*, a form of history as its title suggests. Here Custance is an historical figure alongside her father and her son Mauricius. In part, then, Chaucer's story is not entirely fictional.

Trivet's account points to Custance – or Constance – as a central figure in the Christianisation of Europe. Her father – Emperor of Rome, centre of the Catholic faith – effects a marriage with the Muslim Sultan of Syria who converts rather than lose her. It is when he insists that the rest of his kingdom follow suit that the trouble begins (218–40). Custance is accompanied on her journey by a multitude of bishops and advisers (253). Later she manages to convert others to the faith, a detail highlighting the religious element that is a thread complicating Chaucer's poem.

Playing with genre

Thus another genre contaminates what was originally a folk or romance tale so that several sets of expectations work together on this hybrid form. Chaucer mingles romance, history, religion and to it adds the voice of a fictional narrator with his own agenda. This is then placed within another fiction, that of the wider dramatic frame. The story itself also becomes part of a story-collection, a genre with its own demands, limits and patterning.

In this way, the tale is an example of how stories operate at a variety of levels. *The Man of Law's Tale* can be read separately from the dramatic frame or disconnected from the story-collection genre. The narrator's influence may, as we shall see, work with or against the drift of the story itself. Expectations clash leading to a variety of readings. Is this a folk tale with a focus upon psychological drama and self-identity? Is it romance masquerading as social commentary upon the role of the family and the place of daughters within it? Is it history or else a religious story? What effect does the knowledge of its analogues have upon interpretation? Does singling out one of these possibilities detract from other important strands of the work?

Chaucer manipulates generic conventions and plays upon what an audience expects from differing types of stories. In the same way, too, he takes several sources and reworks them to produce something new. This fracturing of rules and codes opens up entirely the notion of form and multiplies possibilities. Chaucer's challenge is to the very nature of writing itself.

Patterns and expectations

If, then, it is important to be aware of the types of stories Chaucer uses, how easy is it to recognise form? Each genre has its own structural pattern, one often revealed by events or attention to detail. In addition, exploration of vocabulary is usually illuminating.

The Second Nun's Prologue offers several important clues about the sort of story she is about to relate. It is, she tells us, a translation of the 'glorious lif and passioun' of the 'mayde and martyr, Seint Cecilie' (VIII,(G), 26–28). It is the story of a virgin martyr, one who suffers for her faith before gloriously dying for it.

In keeping with hagiographical tradition, this will be a narrative of stark contrasts. The Second Nun opens by noting the ease with which we forget heaven. We concentrate on pleasure, live in 'ydelnesse' instead of 'bisynesse'. This opposition is embedded through the repetition of each word (5/7/10/14/17/22/24) and also expanded by a contrast between 'slouthe' (19) and 'roten slogardye' (17). The narrative delineates good and evil. Our battle is against sin in the tempting form of 'the feend' (7/13/34).

Just in case anyone misses the strong didactic intent of this genre, in traditional style, the Second Nun explores, at length, the meaning of a name. The narrator reminds us that the qualities inherent in Cecilia's name are reflected in her story (86). Cecilia means 'heaven's lily', a symbol equated with chastity and ever busy with God's work (85–119).

The pattern of action is simplistic and the plot highly reductive. A holy childhood and a vow of virginity results in a 'trial'. Here the saint refutes paganism and expounds on the teachings of the Church. Her death is ordered and causes great physical suffering, but bodily pain is offset by spiritual glory. Terminology is self-evidently religious and focused upon an explication of doctrine and/or the promise of eternal life to those who embrace the faith.

Several of Chaucer's other tales are *fabliaux*, a form exemplified early on with the tales of the Miller and the Reeve. A cursory glance at the plots of each soon reveals the format. In the first, an old man marries a young woman who cuckolds him with a young lover. Both the husband and another rival are deceived by an elaborate plan designed to make fools of them. In the second, a miller jealously guards the virtue of his daughter. He apparently outwits a pair of students sent to prevent his notorious thieving of the corn he grinds. They, in turn, trick him, one taking the maidenhead of his daughter and the other having sex with his wife.

The *fabliau* form is saturated by indecency. Terminology is colloquial, prosaic and often lewd or obscene. Scatalogical detail is important. In *The Miller's Tale*, Absolon is mocked for his dislike of 'fartyng' (I(A), 338), a factor exploited when he begs a kiss from his beloved Alison. He kisses her 'naked ers/Ful savourly, er he were war of this' (3734–35). Later, he is duped into kissing Nicholas who puts out 'his ers' in readiness and 'leet fle a fart/As great as it had been a thonder-dent' (3805–08).

Alan and John, the two protagonists of *The Reeve's Tale*, are students from the north, a dialect that Chaucer uses to comic effect in the story. The details of the plot quickly accumulate. While Alan 'had swonken [been on the job] al the longe nyght' with the miller's daughter (I(A), 4235), his friend concocts a plan to ensure that when his wife 'wente out to pisse' (4215) she would end up in his bed. There 'on this goode wyf he leith on soore./So myrie a fit ne hadde she nat ful yoore [she hadn't had such a good time for ages];/ He priketh harde and depe as he were mad' (4229–31). This down-to-earth vocabulary is replicated in many similar stories.

Storytelling

Thus, recognising form is easy. What is far more difficult to establish, however, is the way in which genre is used by Chaucer in *The Canterbury Tales*. Why does he employ so many different types of story in this collection? Most collections of his time had a central theme holding together a diversity of tales. Or, else, all tales in the collection were bound by a single genre, such as epic, romance or courtly love poems. Others grouped stories within a specific framework as in a dream vision or other dramatic devices.

The *Tales* does not directly conform to any of these generic codes. Unfinished, it is partially held within an incomplete frame, that of the storytelling contest itself. It is possible to identify certain themes within the collection – love and marriage, knowledge and authority, social commentary – but no one idea unites it. Instead, Chaucer offers a diversity of themes, ideas and dramas in a dazzling and varied array of tales. What, then, is his intention?

It is possible that he simply wished to explore the nature of genre itself. As such, if there is any over-arching 'theme' at all it is, perhaps, Chaucer's confrontation with the purpose and art of writing, or what it might mean to be an author.

For Chaucer's use of story is not as simple as it first appears. Just as he fractures audience expectations by shifting and distorting a chosen tale's analogues, so, too, he sometimes subtly alters anticipated generic patterns.

Distilling the form

With *The Second Nun's Tale* we apparently receive a perfect replica of a saint's life complete with all the features we explored earlier. Yet, within the space of only three verses, Cecilia's entire childhood and youthful marriage have been described. A short exchange between Cecilia and her husband is swiftly followed by teaching and conversions. The tale's climax is, of course, Cecilia's confrontation with the prefect and her 'glorious' death. Even this, however, is relatively brief with greater emphasis upon her scornful replies rather than the careful explication of God's Word that we might anticipate.

There is little opportunity for us to empathise with Cecilia or her plight. Her scathing rejection of paganism may be morally correct but her zeal is intimidating. What Chaucer seems to do is to take the genre of hagiography and condense it. This streamlining deliberately sharpens its didactic intent and, simultaneously, distorts it. As a vehicle for religious instruction its purpose is crystal clear. Yet even a medieval audience would surely have recognised its complete lack of human focus. Thus, Chaucer twists the conventions of the genre to highlight its intrinsically reductive nature.

A similar process appears to be at work in *The Monk's Tale*. The Monk promises a moral story 'or two, or three' (VII, 1968), a series of tragedies based upon the medieval notion of the vagaries of Fortune. Many of the poems he cites are exceptionally brief: a few lines on Lucifer or Adam. Whatever their length, all recount the same plot whereby someone at the height of their power falls into adversity at the turn of Fortune's wheel (1991–98).

The tales themselves are detailed with style and vigour. Nevertheless, their repetition ensures the Knight's interruption. He begs the Monk to stop depressing him, a sentiment echoed by Harry Bailly (2788–89). Harry claims there is little point in continuing when the only thing keeping his audience awake is the jangling of the bells on his horse's bridle. The Monk declines Harry's request for another story (2780–2803). Instead, we hear, in complete contrast, the complex, moral but entertaining tale of the Nun's Priest.

This is more than an amusing interlude in the dramatic frame. It calls attention to the types of tales told. Harry has asked for stories that both entertain and instruct, as we saw in the opening section. The disparate series offered by the Monk is moral but tedious. His tragedies are taken from 'olde bookes' (1974) and are 'ensamples trewe and olde' (198) that warn against the transitory nature of earthly things such as prosperity and achievement. The Monk proves his point by heaping example upon example so that the didactic intent is emphasised to the exclusion of all else.

Chaucer, then, takes a particular genre, that of tragedy, and shapes it through an instructive narrative. Its source is both written and oral (here told by the Monk). The tradition of instruction is though 'ensamples' taken from earlier versions, a

Genre and Story

process of 'auctoritee' to which we shall return in the final section. Here though, Chaucer explores the entire nature of storytelling, opening it up to question and review.

Juxtaposition and contrast

Manipulation of audience expectation can also occur within a particular generic code itself. One way to achieve this is through the endings of the poems, a point explored in more detail later. Another is via the use of language.

The prosaic terminology that characterises the *fabliaux* is juxtaposed with a surprise element in *The Miller's Tale*. Nicholas is depicted as an accomplished courtly lover with his sweet words and wonderful singing voice (I(A), 3305–06). He speaks the language we recognise as belonging to courtly love, telling Alison that 'deerne [hidden/secret] love' (3278) drives him. If she cannot requite it, he will die (3280–81). He asks for 'mercy' until she grants him his desire (3288).

This elevated vocabulary is replicated in the terminology of Absolon, his inept rival for Alison's affections. Powdered and scented, he stands at Alison's window to tell her of the love-sickness that prevents him from eating (3698–3707). For the sake of true love he appeals for her 'grace' and her 'oore' [mercy] (3726).

This is offset, however, by a coarseness that is more typical of the genre. As Nicholas sweet-talks Alison, he pats her 'aboute the lendes [loins] weel' (3304) and clasps her thighs (3279). At the same time, 'he caughte hire by the queynte' (3276), an obscenity that is compounded by his puns on 'to die' and 'spille' [colloquialisms depicting orgasm] (3278/81). A clear physical element exists alongside the distant, formal notion of courtly love. Alison struggles away, instructing him to keep his hands to himself (3285–87) but it is a token protest.

Absolon also speaks the words of courtly love. Yet he introduces a low, corporeal element – albeit accidentally – with his bathetic admission that he feels faint and sweats, and yearns for her 'as doth a lamb after the tete' (3703–05).

This physicality is further explored towards the end of the tale with Absolon's misdirected kiss, the naked buttocks thrust out of the window, the fart and the branding of Nicholas's 'towte' [bum]. Clearly this juxtaposition of the physical and the spiritual intensifies the comedy. But is there an additional reason for its conclusion?

Opening up to question

The Miller's Tale is preceded by *The Knight's Tale*, an elaborate story of epic proportions and courtly love. Its high theme is matched by its serious diction. To follow it up with a low-life *fabliau* about ordinary, primarily sexual love offers a perfect contrast in the dramatic frame that loosely binds the *Tales*. But is does not fully account for the playing with genre just encountered.

There, Chaucer allows the abstract and spiritual notion of courtly love to be contaminated by the physical, by sex and bodily functions. In this way he is able to suggest that the ideal – represented in *The Knight's Tale* – is hopelessly distanced from everyday reality, that it is potentially outmoded and certainly unrealistic. Interestingly, Nicholas is the successful lover, one who blends courtly love language and physical action. His elegant speech is a charade designed to achieve his aim of 'deerne' love; it is a ploy to get Alison into bed. Thus Chaucer stretches this genre to its limits to produce a humorous tale that, nevertheless, questions the very purity of the courtly ideal invoked in the previous story in the collection.

Creating a gap

The neat resolutions of the *fabliaux* with their simplistic morals are undoubtedly part of their generic code. The proverb at the end of *The Reeve's Tale* is translated as 'He who does evil needn't expect good' (I(A), 4320). The miller of the story is a liar and a cheat. What he receives is payment of the same kind. This notion of rough justice is replicated in *The Miller's Tale* where John's jealous care of his wife is 'rewarded' with her adultery. Nicholas outwits him and also fools Absolon for which he is branded 'in the towte' (I(A),

3853). It is, however, John's punishment that indicates a more problematic response to such tales.

This is a story that has stressed coarse humour, trickery and the physical. Its conclusion is entirely in keeping with that – with emphasis upon sex, the buttocks, and the climax of Nicholas's almost forgotten plot. John is duly waiting in one of the three 'Noah's Arks' he has built for each of them in preparation for the second flood Nicholas has warned him is to come. He sits there, hanging in the rafters while his lodger and his wife enjoy themselves in the marital bed. When he hears Nicholas cry out for water for his scalded buttocks, he assumes it is the signal to cut himself loose.

Plunged to earth, he not only breaks his arm but finds himself the object of great amusement. Despite his attempts to interrupt and explain, Nicholas and Alison tell all the neighbours of 'his' mad plot to prepare for the flood. The word spreads. His injury is ignored as 'his harm' is turned 'unto a jape' and everyone 'gan laughen at this stryf' (3842/49).

Without doubt this is a story of 'game' as required by Harry Bailly. Its corresponding 'solaas' is typical of its genre but less convincing. Morality is inverted as an old man's 'unnatural' love for his young wife is punished. The final lines dismissively summarise events where she is 'swyved' (the equivalent of our contemporary 'f' word) by one man and kissed on 'hir nether ye' by another (3850–52). The last line is especially abrupt: 'This tale is doon, and God save al the route [company]!' (3854), closing down any potential protest or deeper consideration of what actually happens.

Yet is laughter an appropriate response? John may be gullible but he is an innocent victim of Nicholas's largely unnecessary plot to secure the affections of his willing wife. Their practical joke results in only a broken arm – this time. Absolon's response to *his* deception is sadistic in the extreme. This is cruel comedy.

Is Chaucer inviting an alternative consideration of events? Does this chosen genre with its up-ending of expected modes of behaviour – ideals established as one example in the earlier *The Knight's Tale* – call attention to what it seems to satirise? Perhaps this carnivalesque inversion of everyday life is more than just fun.

Maybe Chaucer's use of this genre is intended to critique the gulf between ideals of behaviour and their practice, the topic of our next section. The very amorality of the *fabliaux* highlights received notions of morality and subjects it to questioning.

Tutorial

Further reading
Read *The Nun's Priest's Tale* and explore the shifts in language created by the courtly diction of the farmyard animals and the mock-heroic style of the whole. Read *The Wife of Bath's Tale* (a fairy tale) or *The Knight's Tale*. Look too at *The Parson's Tale*.

Study tips
1. Ask if you can tape tutorials to help you re-order your notes.

2. Always try to speak in class: prepare a list of queries or areas of concern in advance.

3. Supplement class work by choosing a couple of areas to explore further.

Discussion points
1. Why does Chaucer consistently undercut our expectations?

2. What is the intent of the *Tales*? How is it to be read?

3. Is Chaucer's main concern with the art of writing?

Assignment topics
1. The telling of a story can be as interesting and entertaining to the reader as the story that is told. Do you agree?

2. When the stories end the problems they explore remain unresolved. How far is this an accurate assessment of the Chaucer texts you have read?

3. If so many of Chaucer's tales are comic, are we to take seriously any critique of his society?

Research suggestions
1. Explore some aspects of the historical background of Chaucer's time. *Starting points*: the internet; Paul Strohm, *Hochon's Arrow* (Princeton, NJ, 1992). *Study tip*: refine your search so that you only call up information about late medieval religion, for example.

2. Extend your research to include information about Chaucer's literary contemporaries. Read some of them. *Starting point*: See p. 116 for the web site *The Middle English Collection*.

3. Choose a favourite tale and read one or two of its analogues. How might it compare to or contrast with Chaucer's version? What might be revealed about the story itself; its form or genre; its development or audience? *Starting point*: Read two analogues to *The Man of Law's Tale* of Custance: Thomas le Chestre's *Emaré* and John Gower's *The Tale of Constance* (in his *Confessio Amantis*). See ed. G. C. Macauley, *John Gower's English Works*, EETS, ES no. LXXXI, Vol I (London, 1900, rep. 1957), 146–73 and eds. Anne Laskaya and Eve Salisbury, *The Middle English Breton Lays* (Michigan, 1995).

5

Speaker and Story

One-minute summary – The question of matching a tale with its teller may be misleading. Some stories work both with *and* against the voice of their tellers. In this chapter we will explore:

- allocating the tale
- setting up the story
- matching the tale
- review of section

Allocating the tale

As well as the question of what type of tale, we need to consider the speaker who delivers that story. Through *The Canterbury Tales* Chaucer develops the notion of a series of conflicting or, at times, simply unreliable voices in the narrative.

Some speakers perfectly match the tales they relate:

1. The Parson offers a serious, didactic sermon.

2. The Miller and the Reeve engage in a quarrelsome dialogue within the dramatic frame which is reflected in their poems.

3. At the same time, the coarse Miller gives us the bawdy tale we might expect of him, one that also demands to be read in conjunction with its apparent obverse *The Knight's Tale*.

The possibility of exploring a fictional narrator's 'personality' to see if it matches the tale told is, however, fraught with problems. Indeed, it may not even be desirable.

Without doubt, Chaucer re-allocated some of his material. The introduction of *The Man of Law's Tale* suggests that he intends to speak in prose, a claim not borne out in his narrative. Many believe that Chaucer originally intended the Man of Law to deliver *The Tale of Melibee*, even though the Chaucer-the-pilgrim character to whom it is assigned jokingly promises us 'som litel thyng in prose' (VII, 937). The only other prose tale is the Parson's where the content seems a perfect match for its speaker.

Others argue that *The Shipman's Tale* was intended for the Wife of Bath. Its equation of sex and money apparently corresponds to Alison's depiction of loveless marriage, tricky women and her comment that 'al is for to selle' (III(D), 414). The Shipman is named as the final speaker of the preceding fragment and promises 'My joly body schal a tale telle' that will wake up the entire company (II(B^1), 1185–87). Yet the next fragment opens with the Wife's shocking *Prologue*.

Some speakers do not appear in the *General Prologue* so the question of 'fit' is clearly redundant. The Second Nun and the Canon's Yeoman are all additions to the *Tales*, while the Nun's Priest merits a mere two line description. Others – the Yeoman, the Plowman, the Sergeant at Law – are described but take no part in the contest. To what extent is any of this significant?

Setting up the story

The fit between story and speaker is, then, a hit and miss affair. Though some match perfectly, others are more problematic. Some tales may even work against the grain so that though the narrator influences the story, it may not be in manner that is immediately apparent.

When the largely anonymous Nun's Priest is asked to speak it is as a result of the Host's dissatisfaction with the Monk's endless round of tragedies. He calls on the Nun's Priest for something that will gladden 'oure hertes' (VII, 2811). At one point the narrator interrupts the story to raise the possibility that women's advice is invariably misleading. His example is the Adam and Eve story, though his own tale also serves to prove the point. He then swiftly backtracks, insisting that his apparent anti feminism is offered only 'in my game' (3262). His invitation is to 'Rede auctours' who deal more directly with such issues for he himself can 'noon harm of no womman divyne' (3266). Twice he reminds us that he is simply telling a story, that these are the words of a cockerel rather than his own (3265) and that 'My tale is of a cok, as ye may heere' (3252).

This apparent digression is, in fact, central to the effect of his tale, something also intimated by his conclusion. His is a beast fable requiring only a simple moral tag. However, the closing lines also point towards the issue raised by his casual aside. To read this tale as the story of 'a cok and a hen' (4329) is only one, reductive level at which it might be interpreted. The Nun's Priest urges us 'Taketh the moralitee' (3430), search for the 'fruyt and lat the chaf be stille' (3433). His implication that there are alternative, deeper meanings to be gleaned is supported by his citation of St Paul's declaration that in all writing there is 'oure doctrine' (3432).

In other words, Chaucer uses this multi-layered tale to display the skills of story-telling generally. He suggests that interpretation may be surface and simplistic. Equally, it may demand a more complex response, one requiring consideration of tone or knowledge of other authors or stories whose views might alter our perspective. In addition, we are invited to recall the role of the fictional narrator whose skill lies – at least, in part – in drawing us in and entertaining us.

When Harry calls for a merry tale this is, at one level, exactly what he receives. Yet, the Nun's Priest sets up his story so that we are also invited to consider its 'sentence' or meaning. This voice relates a tale that is beast fable, mock-epic and a discussion of courtly love and medieval marriage. Its kaleidoscopic shifts unsettle the genre. Thus, Chaucer reminds us of some of the problems inherent in writing.

Chaucer's focus is, therefore, upon openness, a multiplicity of viewpoint. The fictional narrator is one way in which this focus might be brought to our attention. *The Pardoner's Tale* is another poem where we see this at work.

Matching the tale

When the Pardoner declares that he always preaches a sermon upon avarice, though he himself is guilty of that sin, we are fully prepared for the tale he relates. His story is of three rioters who make a pact to seek out and kill 'Death', he who has killed thousands before them. The three are blood brothers, revellers and gamblers whose language is abrupt and full of oaths. Such blasphemy indicates their total disregard of heavenly grace and salvation, even though they are sorely in need of redemption. The story builds upon this foundation. 'Death' comes to them in the form of an old, gentle man desperate for someone willing to exchange 'his youthe for myn age' (VI(C), 724).

The three treat the old man with disdain, their contempt displayed in threats and orders to tell them where to find Death. When he indicates an oak tree nearby, they rush towards a pile of gold, its immense visual attraction indicating the moral blindness of the three. What they seek is personal gain, a selfish avarice that leads to each trying to outwit the other and dying in the process.

Thus the Pardoner relates a sermon-story against sin, exactly as he promised. It is what we might expect of one whose occupation is to absolve sin, to 'sell' salvation and pardon. The Pardoner's authority comes from the Church. Yet he abuses it for he takes part of the proceeds for himself. He confesses this on more than one occasion (427–34/439–61). His skill lies in instilling guilt in his audience so that they might come forward and receive pardon. Yet he himself is seemingly oblivious of his own need (a similar idea is proposed by David:1976. See Appendices).

The Pardoner's sermon centres on the necessity for spiritual grace and its potential availability to all (even to the rioters) if only they might recognise it. The three are oblivious of the clues Death offers to his identity. The old man wanders the earth citing 'Hooly Writ' (742) that he knows will be ignored. In his farewell to the trio – 'God be with yow' (748) – is a veiled intimation that they will be in need of such help. Equally he reminds them that they ought to treat him respectfully, as they themselves might expect to be treated when they are old – 'if that ye so longe abyde' (747). He speaks to them of the redemptive power of Christ (766–67) before finally indicating the (literal) location of Death.

Undoubtedly through this voice Chaucer is able to criticise his own time's spiritual or moral values and the corruption of its Church. But after the Pardoner's confession, his tale becomes more than a simple match between teller and tale. Instead, our reading is intertextual where each works both with and against the other.

The Pardoner offers a sermon designed as a trick to extort money, exactly as he has warned. Equally there is a further possibility that his tale invites us to re-read the *Prologue* and reconsider the voice that is presented there.

In contrast to the Wife of Bath, the Pardoner's revelations seem deliberate. He recounts his trickery with clarity and ease. He claims 'First I pronounce' (335); 'Thanne shewe I forth' (347); 'Thanne have I' (350); 'Taak kep' (360); 'Heere is' (372); 'But shortly myn entente I wol devyse' (23), and so on. The constructions are marked by colons and semi-colons. This man is an effective public speaker. Though he reveals his innermost nature, he never loses control of that public *persona* or his rhetoric.

Are we to assume then that he is lying? On the contrary, since his ideas are so well elaborated and because they so compound the complexities of his subsequent sermon that we must surely judge it as truth. What then is Chaucer's intent?

The figure of Death is a despairing one. He longs to die so desperately that he will gladly exchange his 'cheste', his valuables for a hair shirt. 'But yet', he adds, 'to me she wol nat do that grace' (734–37). His despair is borne of an inability to find salvation, even though he realises that material gain is worthless beside the spiritual.

Perhaps this story is an additional commentary upon the Pardoner. Like Death, he reveals his true identity to the world. Like Death too, the Pardoner lacks all grace and is seemingly denied its possibility. Though his credibility is destroyed (and that of the institution he represents), his audiences fall for the same old tricks and seemingly fail to recognise him for what he is.

In this way, his sermon has a particular resonance. His tale is an invitation to re-read the Pardoner and, with it, to perhaps recognise our own culpability in permitting him to get away with his actions. Once again, then, Chaucer, multiplies perspective and possibility.

Review of section

In this section we have seen how:

1. Chaucer distorts sources and generic codes in a variety of ways, in order to challenge our expectations.

2. Individual tales vary in the extent to which they 'rely' upon a fictional speaker to make them work.

3. Stories can work both with *and* against the voices of their speakers.

4. These techniques open up narrative and multiply perspective.

Tutorial

Further reading
The Wife tells a fairy story: why? Re-examine her *Prologue* in its light. Look too at the *Prologue* and *Tale* of the *Canon's Yeoman*.

Progress questions
1. How might genre affect our reading?

2. What part does audience expectation play in reading these tales?

3. List some of the ways in which teller and tale might be connected.

Study tips
1. Choose your assignment topic as soon as you can.

2. Once you've decided, ask for an individual reading list or some extra advice.

3. Volunteer for a class presentation on your chosen assignment if possible.

Revision hints
1. Draw up a revision web of themes/topics/influences ready for exploration.

2. Use charts/highlighters/headings/visual cues to weigh up opposing notions or contrasting critical arguments.

3. Make small key cards with topic titles or key questions on to help you revise.

Research suggestions
1. Read, research and explore some medieval dream-visions. *Starting points*: Chaucer's *House of Fame*; William Langland's *Piers Plowman*; the anonymous *Pearl* poem.

2. Read, research and explore some medieval romance tales. Compare them to the folk-romances narrated in the *Tales* by the Clerk and the Man of Law. *Starting points*: ed. Donald B. Sands, *Middle English Romances* (Exeter, 1966, rep. 1997).

3. Read Chaucer's *The Legend of Good Women* where the narrator is commissioned to tell a particular set of tales. Then read his 'originals' in Ovid, *Metamorphoses* (see Penguin edition).

6

Exemplary and Idealised Women

One-minute summary – At first glance Chaucer presents us with ideals of women who are meek, silent, passive and examples of holy perfection. These figures are offered as examples of ideal behaviour. The ideal is institutionalised by reference to the Bible, to Church teachings, to books and 'masculine' authority. The ideal is often affirmed via the narrator who places the subject of his story within an allusive and religious framework. Chaucer begins to use the narrator to open up a gap in the narrative itself. In this chapter we will explore:

- the ideal
- inner and outer virtue
- framing and idealising
- clarifying it

The ideal

When the Parson calls for the avoidance of the sin of lechery, he links it to the preservation of the sacrament of marriage. What he esteems above all is chastity, something that, he argues, is attainable both in and out of marriage (X(I), verse 915).

- *Chastity* – is defined as cleanliness of heart, mind and body. It forms an ideal of behaviour for men and, especially, women, one founded in and perpetuated by the Church.

The dissemination of this ideal was through clerical teaching, patristic writing and a wealth of other literature. As a result, its influence upon medieval life was huge.

In marriage each partner's body was said to belong to the other so that the three conditions of that union might be fulfilled. Sex – legitimated only by marriage – was for procreation, the avoidance of lust or fornication, and payment of the marital 'dette'. The 'dette' was a duty to yield up your body to the other, even if this was against 'hir likynge and the lust of hire herte' (v.935–941).

According to the teachings of St Peter, a married woman should be subject to her husband in obedience and meekness. She should be moderate in eating, drinking, speech and deed, and 'mesurable' in dress and 'contenaunce' [expression] (v.940). Warning against women taking pride in their beauty, the Parson insists they should be sober in dress at all times (v.930). He cites the proverbs of Solomon in support of this idea; a vain woman's body is comparable to a ring of gold through the nose of a sow. Just as the sow roots in filth, so, too, beauty is said to be rooted in the filth of a sinful body (v.155). There were also prohibitions against all kinds of excessive speech, such as gossip, swearing, nagging, lying or betraying secrets (v.495–510/600–650).

The Parson's Tale informs us of a crucial medieval ideal governing and circumscribing attitudes towards women. In short, a wife must be 'mesurable in lookynge and in berynge and in lawghynge [laughing], and discreet in alle hire wordes and hire dedes' (v.935). She may well be admired for her beauty, but she must also be meek, mild, modest and patient in all things.

Inner and outer virtue

Thus, outer beauty was regarded as worthless unless it also matched an ideal of inner virtue. Chaucer presents us with a handful of women in the *Tales* who are admired – apparently – for exactly this.

Cecilia
Cecilia, for example, is special by nature of her holiness. She is raised as a Christian in a pagan world, and prays unceasingly to remain a virgin (VIII(G), 119–26). The summary of her as 'ful devout and humble in hir corage' (131) conforms to an important standard.

Custance

Custance, too, is not only beautiful but full of 'goodnesse' so that her unparalleled virtue is broadcast by the merchants as far afield as Syria (II(B^1), 158–60). Though not a saint like Cecilia, her heart is a 'chambre of hoolynesse' (167) and 'To alle hire werkes vertu is hir gyde' (164). She is charitable, humble, a 'mirour of alle curteisye' (166). All love her who meet her. Exiled in Northumberland, she is 'so diligent, withouten slouthe', making it her business to serve everyone (530–32). The people weep in recognition of her virtue when she is led to trial, falsely accused of murder (624), an allegation only arising in envy of 'hire perfeccioun' (583).

Griselda in *The Clerk's Tale*

In *The Clerk's Tale*, Griselda is also young and lovely. More importantly, for 'vertuous beautee' she is the fairest in the world (IV(E), 214). She is without 'likerous luste' (214), drinks well water rather than wine and works hard, attentively caring for her aged father (332–34) 'in greet reverence and charitee' (221). She tends the sheep, toils in the fields and spins wool. Griselda is obedient, diligent and humble, both as a wife and a daughter (230–31/600–04). Walter's choice of her as bride – despite her poor origins – is based on a recognition of her exemplary 'wommanhede', the way her 'chiere' or appearance matches deed (241). Her inner virtue, then, conforms to that ideal we have just explored. Within her breast is enclosed a 'rype and sad corage' (220), a steadfast and profound integrity. When he marries her, all adore her.

Griselda's reputation spreads far. She is commended for her virtue, discretion, kindness, eloquence and dignity (440–27). With her wise judgement, she is able to bring peace and harmony to the land (428–41). In short, she is a 'benigne, verray, feithful mayde' (343).

An ideal of feminitiy

Though only ordinary, these women offer us an important ideal of femininity. They are intended – by their narrators, at least – to give example to others. Cecilia's active defence of her virginity as a

Bride of Christ ensures that she becomes a saint. The behaviour of the lowly peasant girl Griselda is so exemplary that it seems as if she was born an empress (IV(E), 396–99).

Custance comes close to sanctity without actually dying for her faith. She converts many of the Northumberland people who wish to emulate her virtue (II(B^1), 535–39/574/683–86), thus adding another dimension to her tale. When she finally returns to Rome, she spends her time in holy deeds (980), living out her days 'In vertu and hooly almus-dede' (1156). Elsewhere, she is described as a 'hooly wyf so sweete' (1129), 'this hooly creature' (1149), and 'this hooly mayden, that is so bright and/sheene' (692).

What Chaucer begins to set up, then, is an exploration of that medieval ideal of womanhood presented to us by men like the Parson. At first glance, each of the women portrayed here conforms to our expectations where ordinary goodness is closely allied to a near-holy perfection. How does Chaucer deepen the impact of these exemplary figures?

Speech and silence, moderation and meekness

Moderation in all things, but especially speech, is a virtue demanded of medieval women. Silence is deemed admirable. If a woman must speak, then it ought to be with humility, meek obedience and a measure of restraint.

Though Custance rarely speaks directly in her own story, she twice offers a lengthy address to her father. On both occasions, her words are exemplary in their meek deference. When he arranges for her to be sent to Syria, she accedes completely to his paternal authority. She begins 'Fader' (274), from then on naming herself as his. She is 'thy wrecched child' (274), 'thy yonge doghter' and 'youre child' (275). She agrees to go to Syria, far from family and friends, because it is her father's will (283–84).

Her final reunion with her father confirms this meekness. Kneeling (1104), she again opens her speech with 'fader' in acceptance of his power, a term she repeats three times in just a few lines (1105/1109/1111). Once more, she is 'youre yonge child' (1105) and 'youre doghter' (1107), an affirmation of her defenceless and subordinate position.

Exemplary and Idealised Women

When Griselda speaks, her words, too, are the epitome of virtuous womanhood delivered with 'reverence, in humble cheere' (IV(E), 298). She swears an oath of allegiance to Walter on their wedding day, that she will never contradict him or show displeasure – either verbally or by a look – whatever might happen (351–57). In keeping with this, she apparently acquiesces in the murder of her own children.

At her first child's death, 'she noght ameved/Neither in word, or chiere, or contenaunce' (498–99). Griselda declares that both she and her baby are Walter's entirely; hers is only to obey (501–11). When she loses her second child, she says 'Naught greveth me at al,/Though that my doughter and my sone be/slayn' (646–48).

So, Griselda patiently accepts the constable's removal of her babies. In 'hire benigne voys', she simply blesses them and requests that they are buried where no animals might disturb the grave (554–72/679–83). Later, cast out in favour of a new bride, she returns to her father's house where she remains silent, meek and discreet, full of 'pacient benyngnytee' (911–31).

Cecilia, in *The Second Nun's Tale*, also begins by addressing her husband with courtesy in 'O swete and wel biloved spouse deere' (VIII(G), 144). Like Griselda, her story *is* marked by direct speech. She tells Valerian that he, too, might see the angel who protects her if he obeys her instructions and allows Urban to baptise him. His safe entry into the hidden world of the Christians is via the 'wordes' of Cecilia herself (180). Later, she similarly instructs Tiburce (294–305) and, speaking 'boldely' (319) preaches to him of the Trinity and Christ's Passion (320–48).

Her words have a totally different effect, however, from the idealised speeches of the previous women. Summoned before the prefect Almachius, she openly laughs at him (562), dismissing his faith and mocking his questions (428–30). Cecilia accuses him of confusion and lying (463–66), sneering at him and his authority (493–511). The text records how 'Thise wordes and swiche othere seyde she' (512).

Cecilia, then, appears to flout the medieval ideal of perfect, meek womanhood. She speaks aggressively and in public, open defiance of masculine authority (rather like the Wife of Bath). How are we intended to respond to her?

Hers is the story of a saint, one who actively defends her faith before paganism. Her identity is not merely female but also explicitly holy. Cecilia is, then, a generic type. As we saw in section two, the influence of genre is sometimes crucial. Here, Cecilia is permitted a confrontational speaking role precisely *because* she is a saint. The genre – hagiography – thus defuses the threat otherwise posed by a woman who refuses to conform to the ideal and be silent.

Framing and idealising

So far, we have explored how women might be presented as exemplary by being described as passive, semi-saintly victims. At the end of the first section, we also worked through the Clerk's narrative strategy, one that placed the subject of his story, Griselda, in a restricting framework. The Man of Law adopts a similar technique.

It is the merchants who, at the start of the poem, pass on the good tidings about Custance's virtue. When they speak what the narrator terms 'the commune voys of every man' (II(B^1), 155), they confirm her value as an object to be prized, something spoken of by men in a voice that – according to the Man of Law – is a truth comparable only to God's (169).

The Man of Law's interruptions add to the idealisation of Custance by framing her as a passive victim of events. When she departs from Rome, he expostulates against the cruelty of Fortune and the unhappy alignment of the planets. Allusions to the destruction of Troy and Thebes, plus attacks on Rome by Hannibal, complete the effect (288–315). What is suggested is that Custance is subject to events beyond her control.

The narrator's terminology also works to establish Custance as a helpless victim deserving of our compassion. She is 'woful', merely a 'mayde' (316/378), is called 'O my Custance' (805) or 'O my Custance, ful of benignytee' (446), the apostrophes intensifying the intended emotional impact. He describes her as a 'sely innocent' (682), an 'innocent' like a lamb led to the slaughter (617–18) where 'Allas!', what might she do (608)? During the trial scene, the narrator again interjects with 'Allas!' and notes how

Custance is without a champion or protector (631–35).

Custance's passivity is implicitly contrasted to the active wickedness of her mothers-in-law who plot to cast her out. These are masculinised or 'feyned' women (362) whose malice is directed against an ideal of virtue represented by Custance herself. Read what the Man of Law has to say about them and ask yourself why he is so vitriolic.

Equating virtue with helplessness and holiness

However, the narrator's most blatant colouring of his tale is centred upon his equation of virtue with both helplessness and holiness. This is an integral link already highlighted in previous sections. Here, he insists that Custance defends herself against attempted rape only through the intervention of the Virgin Mary. Thus, 'Crist unwemmed [unblemished]' kept Custance (924).

This is reinforced by yet another interjection raging against the foul sin of lechery and the evil of men. How, he asks, might a woman defend herself against such a threat? How did David defeat Goliath, he continues, or Judith kill Holofernes (925–45)? What is affirmed in this lengthy tirade is that the woman is passive, her success due only to God's assistance.

In the narrator's far from humble opinion, Custance's sufferings are finally alleviated simply because the Virgin Mary shaped it so (950–52/977–78). Yet these interjections are suspect. The text raises a host of questions: why does Custance conceal her identity on so many occasions (a point to which we shall return); how does she survive twice being cast adrift in a rudderless ship; how is she finally saved? These are the questions the text does not directly answer, preferring to leave them blank.

The Man of Law pre-empts those questions and moves swiftly to offer his own views on the matter, views that firmly restrain the potential of Custance to act as an independent agent in her own story. Instead, his offerings contain her within a restricting narrative framework; they keep her passive and good.

So, he protests at length, it is the Virgin Mary who ends her tribulation, an interpretation that neglects the fact of her rescue by the Roman fleet. Equally, she survives at sea because it is God's will, an idea he attempts to reinforce through a string of similar comparisons: Daniel in the lion's den; Jonah in the belly of the whale; Mary of Egypt in her desert exile. The list is exhaustive and only makes us wary of his reductive suggestions (470–504). Of course, Chaucer may well be opening up gaps in the narrative here that he exploits in an entirely different way, using the voice of the fictional narrator as a screen. We shall return to this shortly.

Clarifying it

The Man of Law insists that Custance's life is worked out through a divine grace that confirms her own goodness (938). He compares her delivery to that of the chosen tribe, the Israelites, adding 'I seye, for this entente,/That right as God spirit of vigour sente/To hem and saved hem out of meschance,/So sente he myght and vigour to Custance' (939–45). What happens is that Custance is constructed *through* a particular narrative stance. She is acted upon by a patriarchal world (represented by her father), by God and by the narrator himself. In this way, Chaucer uses his narrators to affirm an *exemplum* [example], one that he himself may not entirely accept.

The ending of *The Man of Law's Tale* is an implausibly fairy-tale one of reconciliation. Alla and Custance weep in each other's arms, a scene so affecting that the narrator claims he may tell no more until tomorrow for he is 'so wery for to speke of sorwe' (1065–71. It is a reunion of such 'blisse' and eternal 'joye' (1075–76), two key terms that are repeated throughout the closing verses. They ride out in joy and gladness (1102) to meet Custance's father. Of that reunion, he asks, who can tell of its 'pitous joye' or the 'joye and blisse' in which they remain (1114–15/1119)? Returned to England, Custance is said to live in quiet joy (1131) and 'blisse' (1140–41).

When the narrator reminds us that earthly joy cannot last (1133), he prepares us for the apparent resolution of this tale. Custance, as we have seen, is an exemplary woman. Part of that excellence is her piety. Thus, we are alerted to a shift in the key terminology of the concluding lines.

However well deserved after her sufferings, her human joy – like all human things – is only transient. Now this 'hooly creature' must return to Rome (1149) to live out her days in virtue and 'hooly' charity (1156). The narrative ends with a commendation to Christ (1161–62) to whom, according to the Man of Law, Custance owes her life. The lesson of the text, then, appears to be affirmation of exemplary (especially female) behaviour, for virtue will guarantee reward in heaven.

The three main portraits studied in this chapter simultaneously affirm that these women are exemplary figures, for us to admire and emulate. Obedient, meek, 'holy', virtuous and largely silent; these are the qualities to which medieval women were taught to aspire.

The final effect, though, is one of distance. We probably cannot accept that to die a virgin martyr, as Cecilia does, is an example to us all (or, accepting the historical distance, even to medieval women), or that Griselda will live happy ever after with her lord, Walter, forgetting his bizarre behaviour of previous years. In addition, these women lack the warmth and humour of a figure like the Wife of Bath or even Alison in *The Miller's Tale*. Instead, they are inhuman ciphers. Their very idealisation makes it difficult for us to empathise with them. Is this presentation accidental?

We already know that Chaucer creates a series of fictional narrators. The process allows him to hide behind them, to open up gaps and ambiguities in the text that, in turn, multiply possibilities, widen perspective and offer the presentation of an ideal that is simultaneously undermined. Within that space, he is free to critique the very codes of behaviour that circumscribe the lives of ordinary medieval people.

It is an ambiguity intimated by the Clerk himself who, at the same time as he offers Griselda as an example to all, reminds us that it would be impossible to emulate as a lesson in wifely humility (VI(E), 114). Chaucer sets up a standard that he then questions, one that, as we shall see in the next chapter, he purposefully clouds and fragments.

Tutorial

Further reading
Read the portrait of Virginia in *The Physician's Tale* or the more

problematic ideal of the Prioress in the *General Prologue*. Look, too, at the fairy-tale ending of *The Clerk's Tale*. What sorts of problems does it raise?

Assignment tips
1. Make sure you keep a card index or some other record of your reading – complete with page numbers – as you go along, rather than trying to reference essays later.

2. Find out early on about your departmental requirements for referencing and keep to their format.

3. Remember that all work requires a complete bibliography. This must include the full details of all works referred to but should also note other texts that you have used more widely and more generally.

Revision hints
1. Rather than simply re-reading chunks of material, aim to make notes. Then make notes on your notes so that you gradually reduce everything to key reminders.

2. Use short snappy titles or mnemonics to help you recall material.

3. Number points: 5 facts about, or 3 questions to raise.

Discussion points
1. Is the only good woman in a Chaucerian text a silent one?

2. How does Chaucer set up the notion of masculine authority? Is that authority always right?

3. Are Chaucer's women abhorrent to a contemporary audience? If so, does it matter?

7

Subverting the Ideal

One-minute summary – Chaucer uses a variety of strategies to raise questions about ideals. He uses ambiguous portraits, undercuts speakers' voices, accumulates ideas, words or phrases, juxtaposes images or styles of language, and uses asides. Chaucer offers us examples of conformity to an ideal only to subvert it. Chaucer elides closure, refusing to answer the questions he raises and so fractures the notion of authority. In this chapter we will discuss:

- raising questions
- meaningful silences
- subversive speech
- autonomous action
- weaknesses in narrative voice
- other possibilities
- compounding the question
- review of section

Raising questions

Does Chaucer always offer us such ideal portraits, or does he raise other questions that undercut that ideal? Let us begin by briefly examining the presentation of Alison in *The Miller's Tale*.

Alison in *The Miller's Tale*
The opening description of Alison is that of a lovely, fresh and natural girl. She is tall with black, arched eyebrows and a mouth as sweet as mead or apples. Quick and playful, she is frequently compared to animals: a colt or kid skipping after its mother, a voice like a swallow, a body as slender as a weasel and soft as ram's wool. She is like a primrose and, in short, 'moore blisful on to see/

Than is the newe pere-jonette tree' (I(A), 3247–48).
Such natural images enhance her beauty and seem admiring.

1. What though is the cumulative effect of comparison to so many animals? Chaucer might be intimating that she is actually base or lustful, and certainly her later behaviour with Nicholas might add to this. Or is she simply innocent and natural?

2. Alison's clothes, too, match her loveliness, but do they also call attention to a certain vanity, a pride in her body that might be viewed as sinful? Look at the way in which her skirt flares over 'hir lendes' [loins] (3237), or her shoes are laced high up her legs (3267). Notice, too, her 'likerous' or flirtatious eye (3244).

3. Similarly, her naturalness is undercut by hints of artifice: a purse adorned with 'latoun', a brassy metal (3251), eyebrows 'ypulled' (3245), and her brooch broad as a 'bokeler', the raised centre of a shield (3266). We are told that she is brighter than a newly minted 'noble' (3255–56). In this loosely structured extract a string of images fight with each other and resist final definition.

The power of accumulated ideas

This is a process enhanced by the juxtaposition of the concluding remarks about her. She is described as lower class, a 'wenche' (3254) or a gay 'popelote [dolly]', fit for any *lord* to have in his *bed* or any *yeoman* to *wed* (3269–70, italics mine). The accumulation of ideas ensures that what at first sight appears to be an approving portrait is rendered less secure, a technique repeated elsewhere. Look at the cumulative effect of the repetition of 'fresshe' May in *The Merchant's Tale*, a word that shifts as the plot is revealed to us.

Meaningful silences

Does Chaucer uphold the traditional division of women as either whores or saints, the old Eve-Madonna split? Or, is the picture more ambiguous than this?

Example

1. In *The Merchant's Tale*, a young girl is brought to bed 'as stille as stoon' (1818). Old Januarie's love-making may be comic but it is also repulsive. The text focuses upon his active and lengthy concentration on his new bride. This is followed by his delighted air the next morning (1819–59). His appearance is repellent with the slack skin of his neck wobbling as he sings and, earlier, the thought of his bristly face rubbing all over her.

2. About May's response the text is tellingly silent. We assume she is the passive recipient of *his* pleasure. In fact, a significant break in the narration at this point highlights this underlying question. It records 'God woot' what May 'thoughte in hir/ herte' when she saw him, adding 'She preyseth nat his pleyyng worth a bene' (1851–54). In part, this interlude is humorous with Januarie talking about what he is going to do and how excellent his performance will be (1828–42). But it also raises questions about the sacrament of marriage and its purpose. What is missing from this depiction of honeymoon bliss is both love and mutual joy. How sympathetic, then, is Chaucer to women's plight in such an arrangement?

It is a question to which we are returned in *The Man of Law's Tale*. The narrator – or is it, in fact, Chaucer's voice? – notes that, though wives are holy, they must submit at night with patience to whatever their husbands' desire by laying 'a lite hir hoolynesse aside' (II(B^1), 713). Elsewhere, the Wife of Bath comments openly upon sex in marriage. To what extent does her voice complicate the issue, do you think?

Subversive speech

Earlier we explored Cecilia's open and confrontational speech. Her challenge was seen as a legitimate one because she is a saint refuting paganism. However, if we re-examine some other, apparently idealised, speeches by women it might be possible to read them differently. Their words may, after all, be more ambiguous than at first appears.

Example
In *The Clerk's Tale* Griselda's meek dialogue is perfectly ideal. On the surface what she says is entirely in keeping with her oath never to contradict Walter. Yet her apparently meek words underscore the cruelty of his actions and carefully absolve her of responsibility; she is merely his possession, someone for whom he displays little love or duty of care. She is apparently unmoved by the slaughter of her children, an act committed 'at youre comandement' (IV(E), 649).

We are reminded of this near the end with Griselda's comment that it is thanks to the tender care of 'youre benyngne fader' – surely ironic – that her children are safe. At this point she breaks off and falls down into a faint (1097–99). Here we see the tremendous personal cost of her refusal to reveal her true feelings or openly castigate Walter for his actions.

Instead, her criticism of Walter – and Chaucer's of an ideal imposed on women – is more subtle. She highlights Walter's appalling cruelty by begging him to avoid tormenting his new 'wife', one nobly raised and who could not endure suffering 'As koude a povre fostred creature', like herself (1042–43).

Griselda also suggests that though she is prepared to walk naked out of the palace, a simple smock would cover the womb of one 'That was youre wyf' (886–89). She reminds both us – and his subjects – that she is mother to his heirs and, as such, deserving of dignity.

Shattering the ideal

The most openly subversive speech, however, comes from the mouth of the Wife of Bath. Later we will explore her open challenge to masculine authority, but let us begin by examining how the presentation of this figure seems to undercut the ideal of femininity that is the theme of this and the previous chapter.

Chastity rejected
In her lengthy and sometimes rambling *Prologue*, Alison rejects the notion of chastity.

Subverting the Ideal

1. She tells us that she has married five husbands and looks forward to the sixth (III(D), 44f–46).

2. Equally, her interpretation of St Paul's command of virginity is that it is merely advice, 'conseille' not instruction (61–70). When Christ spoke of chastity or 'continence', she reasons, He was addressing only those who would live perfect, saintly lives (105–12), not ordinary people like herself.

3. At the same time she publicly declares her joy in the physicality of love with 'I was a lusty oon' (605) with 'a coltes tooth' (602) and, according to her husbands, 'the beste *quoniam*' in town (608).

Pleasure in sex

This shocking revelation shatters the notion of women as meek or holy. Alison admits to three features that indicate her pleasure in sex.

1. She has a birthmark, 'Venus seel' (604) plus another 'Martes mark' both on her face and in a more intimate place (619–20).

2. She has gap-teeth (603), a sign of lechery.

3. She confesses that, dominated by Venus the planet of love (609–10), she can never withdraw 'My chambre of Venus from a good felawe' (618).

Subverting masculine domination

Alison also details at length what she said to her husbands to ensure her domination of them (224–394). Hardly meek and obedient, she 'chidde hem spitously' (223). What the Wife offers is advice to other women, to speak boldly and accuse their men of things they have never done (226–28). No man, she says, could ever swear and lie as a woman can. She spends her time complaining and accusing (385–90), even in bed at night (406–09), an endless round of nagging and chiding that she insists she would not cease even if the Pope himself sat at their table. In this way, she outdid them 'word for word' (419–22).

Chaucer uses her voice to subvert a masculine-dominated view of the world, one that depicts woman as frail and passive. Of course, since her portrait is also a comic one, he may, in fact be doing the very opposite of this and drawing attention to the ways in which the Wife's attributes match those of women in medieval antifeminist tracts: duplicitous, sexually voracious, vain, and disobedient.

Autonomous action

Speech is, though, only one way of subverting idealised depictions of women. The *behaviour* of the Wife of Bath is equally significant. In her advice to other women, Alison offers a list of activities that will ensure 'maistrie' over men.

1. By accusing her husbands of lechery, she is able to go out freely, even at night, all under the guise of searching out what she alleges are her husbands' partners in adultery ((III(D), 397–98).

2. She travels on pilgrimages or processions, attends weddings, plays, and parties (555–59). The Wife dresses up in her finery, quoting St Paul on why women should dress moderately. She is dismissive of such commandments, saying that she cares nothing for these proscriptions and comparing herself to a sleek cat out on the tiles (337–56).

3. In springtime, she goes from house to house gossiping (544–53) for she loves 'to be gay' (545) and free of her husband. Women, she adds, dislike men who confine them. She insists on her right to act 'at large' or as she wishes (322).

Alison flaunts herself in defiance of medieval codes of behaviour for women. Does Chaucer intend us to take seriously her *Prologue*? What are we to make of her comments about sex? She acts the part of the grieving widow at her fourth husband's funeral because, she says, that is what wives are expected to do (558-89). In fact, she spends her time lusting after Jankyn their parish clerk, twenty to her forty. All she can think of, as she follows the funeral bier, is Jankyn's lovely legs (596-601).

In bed, she demands that her husbands make love to her. Though she feigns enjoyment, she reveals her dislike of old 'bacon' [flesh]. Her aim is 'wynnyng', to use sex to gain money in a manner that takes literally the notion of marital 'dette' (407-18). Alison teases them, nagging then kissing them, urging patience and falsely promising that her '*bele chose*' is for them alone (431-50).

Her behaviour calls sharp attention to the nature of many medieval marriages where Church teachings on its sacramental value deny the possibility of love and enjoyment. The attitude of women like the Wife, Alison in *The Miller's Tale* or May in *The Merchant's Tale* is, thus, significant. Softening criticism through the use of humour (for all are comic poems), Chaucer is, nevertheless, able to bring into focus issues relevant to his own time.

Weaknesses in narrative voice

Chaucer also does this in other, more serious tales broadening the scope of his critique and deepening its impact. The Man of Law is at pains to uphold an ideal of womanhood and to contain the subject of his story in a close narrative framework. There are, however, times when this framework is fractured. In this way, Chaucer is able to open up perspective and alert us to the possibility of a different viewpoint.

The length of the Man of Law's interjections to explain how Custance survived her exiles at sea make us suspect his rhetoric, especially when he fleetingly concedes on two occasions that 'She dryveth forth into oure occian' ($II(B^1)$, 505) and how in the sea 'She dryveth forth hir weye' ((875). Both constructions intimate a more active independence where *Custance* is responsible for her own fate.

Several moments in the tale invite further exploration.

1. An attempted rape fails because Christ keeps her safe. So says the Man of Law in a lengthy interlude, full of apostrophes, on the weakness of women. Yet, he also admits that 'with hir struglyng wel and myghtily', *she* pushes her assailant overboard (921–22).

2. Custance also inexplicably chooses to conceal her identity when she is saved by others, even when rescued by her own uncle and safely installed in her aunt's house in Rome (524–26/971–3/ 981–81/1084–85).

3. At the same time, it is Custance who orchestrates the final reunion scenes. Twice she uses her son, Maurice, to effect the meetings with Alla and her father. The Man of Law draws attention to exactly this even as he attempts to raise the possibility of doubt concerning its truth. He says 'som men' would say it was at her request Maurice is taken to meet Alla, who subsequently recognises Custance's likeness in the child's face. He cannot detail every circumstance (1009–11). Here the narrator's silence is unusual. Equally, he adds that some would say that it was Maurice who sent an invitation to Custance's father. The Man of Law prefers to believe that Alla issued it (1086–92).

What remains is a series of gaps or textual absences, silences that invite our speculation. Thus, Chaucer opens up the possibility that Custance is more independent than the narrator's exemplary narrative permits.

Other possibilities

Chaucer a friend to women?
To what extent, then, might Chaucer be considered a friend to women? It may be impossible to judge, especially when tales seem to end on a note of closure confirming patriarchal authority.

1. So, Cecilia's aggressive confrontation with Almachius ends with emphasis upon her sanctity, as might be expected of hagiography.

2. Yet Custance, too, despite moments of ambiguity in the text, is brought back within the confines of the narrative frame, within family and society.

3. For Griselda, a fairy-tale ending seems to elide all possibility of subversion. She is re-appropriated as Walter's object, his followers, once again, stripping and re-clothing her in a golden gown, before crowning her just as they did at the start (VI(E), 1114–20).

Something humorous or something shocking?
Though the *Wife of Bath's Prologue* presents us with an entirely different portrait from the ideal, we have already raised the question of its intent. Exactly how rebellious is she? On the one hand, Chaucer invites us to laugh at Alison's idiosyncratic vision of the world. Well-versed in marriage, she admits to having chosen her husbands for both financial security and their 'nether purs' [masculine endowment] (III(D), 446). Her coarse asides are highly entertaining. She makes frequent, if coy, reference to her '*bele chose*', '*quoniam*' or 'chambre of Venus'. We laugh at her description of how her struggle for 'maistrie' results in a literal fight with Jankyn. We are amused, too, by her numerous digressions as she conversationally reveals herself to us. The tale she promises is a long time arriving and she often loses the thread of her monologue.

The flaunting of her sexuality is, however, more problematic. We may be shocked by her intimate confession of how she will freely use 'myn instrument' (149–50), boasting that her husband shall have it morning and night (152). She laughs when she recalls how she made her men work at night (201–02). She adds that she never loved in moderation but 'evere folwede myn appetit' whatever the man looked like (622–25).

The Wife a virago?
Her delight in the body might be read as an integral feature of a presentation of a virago, the epitome of the very anti feminist books she takes exception to Jankyn reading. She cheats, dresses up, gossips and answers back. Has Chaucer created a depraved

monster, proof of women's 'known' treachery and insatiable sexual appetite? Or is she simply comic, not to be taken seriously?

A case for compassion?
It is equally possible that Alison is, in fact, intended to arouse our compassion. Her innocent chatter hints at a longing for love. She likes any man so long as 'he liked me' (625) and cries 'Allas, allas! That evere love was synne!' (614). Yet she chooses husbands for their wealth and equates sex with money, as we have seen. She argues that by playing hard to get women increase men's desire for 'Greet prees at market maketh deere ware,/And to greet cheep is holde at litel prys' (522–23), and then chooses Jankyn for love. Chaucer opens up questions that he then deliberately elides.

Compounding the question

The closing moments of *The Clerk's Tale* also hint at further possibilities. Griselda's son refuses to 'assay' or test his own wife (IV(E), 1138). The narrator himself, when explicating the lesson of his text, declines to offer Griselda as an *exemplum* of how wives should behave (1142–44). His remark – that this would be 'inportable' (1144) – points towards a recognition that such behaviour, however ideal, is impossible in real life. Yet, in the next breath, the Clerk confesses his admiration for women like Griselda, the more prized because of their rarity (1162–69).

Elusive meanings
Chaucer heaps possibility upon possibility here, each less definitive than the last. The tale slides away from us. Having raised questions about marriage and the prescriptive codes of behaviour confining women, Chaucer then refuses to answer them. Thus, he moves from the implausibility of a happy ending to an intimation that the story contains a moral lesson – that we should all, regardless of gender, accept adversity as part of God's plan for us. The Clerk's next words about Griselda undermine that lesson while the sudden and inexplicable appearance of 'L'envoy of Chaucer' (1176) turns the entire poem on its head.

Who is this Envoy? At first glance it appears as if the Clerk continues speaking. The song, though, dispels that notion. It is offered on behalf of the Wife of Bath and her 'followers' (1169–72) and advocates a form of behaviour far removed from Griselda's patient humility. It calls upon wives to speak out, to refuse to allow clerks to 'write of yow a storie' like this one. Do not suffer in silence, it urges, but be as fierce as the tiger. Offer your husband not reverence but jealousy and 'crabbed [angry] eloquence' (1203). Display your beauty or if you have none then spend freely. In short, have fun! (1189–1212).

Is Chaucer serious here or is this an amusing interlude to lighten the appalling – if restrained – brutality of the tale itself? What is important is the continual erosion of closure. We are presented with shifting viewpoints that clash and seem to cancel each other out. Though Chaucer's final opinion is unclear, he has at least opened up a range of possibilities and alternatives. Perhaps it does not finally affirm the ideal at all.

The last word on the subject is given to Harry Bailly whose opinion as we saw in the opening chapter is notoriously unreliable and reductive. So, when he wishes his wife had heard *The Clerk's Tale* – presumably so she might emulate Griselda's exemplary behaviour despite the Clerk's own advice – we can at least be sure that he has misread it (1212c–d).

Subversion of authority?

If there is subversion at all perhaps it lies not in the questions themselves but in Chaucer's deliberate policy of undermining *all* authority, including that – as we see here – of writing. This is the subject of our concluding section.

Review of section

In this section we have seen

1. how Chaucer apparently reflects an ideal about women with examples of their good behaviour

2. how Chaucer simultaneously undercuts that ideal and interrogates it

3. how in this way he fractures the notion of masculine authority (including writing) from whence the ideal comes.

Tutorial

Further reading
Explore what Custance says to her father at the start and end of *The Man of Law's Tale*. Might it be seen as challenging or implicitly critical? Follow through the repetition of 'fresshe May' in *The Merchant's Tale*. What is its cumulative effect?

Discussion points
1. Do you think that Chaucer could be described as a friend to women or one sympathetic to their plight?

2. Is Chaucer's eliding of closure ultimately a problem for his audience?

3. Would you say that Chaucer is a radical or a conservative author?

Exam tips
1. Read between the lines of exam questions. They may not be worded as you expect.

2. Before you start answering, draw up a plan or a series of quick-fire headings.

3. Keep to the time limit for individual questions, leaving them unfinished if necessary.

Assignment topics
1. How much substance is there in feminist readings of Chaucer's work?

2. The passive saintly ideal is an example for all women to follow and is presented uncritically by Chaucer in his tales about women. Do you agree?

3. In Chaucer questions of power and gender are inextricably mixed. Discuss.

Research suggestions
1. Examine some representations of medieval women, both ordinary and 'cult' figures like the Virgin Mary or Mary Magdalene. *Starting points*: art galleries or museums; churches and cathedrals; illuminated manuscripts or medieval *Books of Hours*.

2. Read and analyse some feminist or gender-based approaches to the work of Chaucer. *Starting points*: **Wider Reading** or web material at the back of this book.

3. Read and discuss/analyse writing by medieval women. How might their work be different from that of men? Does any of it offer a challenge to the authority of men or their writing traditions? *Starting point*: ed. Alexandra Barratt, *Women's Writing in Middle English* (London and New York, 1992).

8

Knowledge and Experience

One-minute summary – Ideals of behaviour affecting the lives of ordinary medieval people were institutionalised via a range of clerical and written authorities. Chaucer shows a clash between knowledge taken from books (written authority) and everyday, experiential knowledge. That clash offers the possibility of a gap between the ideal and its practice. In this chapter we will explore:

- ▶ institutionalising authority
- ▶ authorising marriage
- ▶ everyday experience
- ▶ a struggle for power
- ▶ a material evidence

Institutionalising authority

The institution of marriage

One of Chaucer's recurring themes in the *Tales* appears to be marriage, a battleground of expectations and practices that, in fact, raises a further crucial element, one integral to medieval life as a whole. This is the conflict between knowledge and experience that we have touched on earlier.

The Parson has much to say on the subject of marriage. His views stem from his own clerical learning, from an accepted and authoritative knowledge. Exploration of them gives us an insight into an area that was, for Chaucer at least, a locus of conflict.

The previous section suggested that it was deemed sinful to engage in sex outside marriage; even within it, the purpose of sex was clearly specified. The Parson also tells us that a man must love his wife in moderation, 'as though it were his suster' and second only to God (X(I), v.860). The institution of marriage is embedded 'in paradys, in the estaat of innocence, to multiplye mankynde to the service of God'. As such, fornication, prostitution, pimping, or other harlotry is a wrong done to Christ who, it is said, owns us body and soul. The Parson warns, too, those married couples seeking only 'flesshly delit' that such pleasure is classified as sin (v.900–05).

Matrimony is established as a sacramental bond whereby deadly sin is transformed into lesser, venial sin. Man must take only one woman just as there is one Church and one God, something that, as we shall see, proves problematical for those like the Wife of Bath who take several partners in their lifetime (v.915–20).

The Parson supports his comments with a range of written authorities like St Paul or St Augustine, plus biblical precedents such as the story of the woman taken in adultery (v.890.900/920/925/930). Here, he is appealing to a tradition involved in the establishment of definitive truth. He is also acting within an institution (the Church itself) that is exceptionally powerful, one whose authority pervaded every aspect of the medieval world.

1. Is it enough, though, to have knowledge of these ideals?

2. What effect did such notions have upon the lives of ordinary people?

3. How might ideals have been promulgated and then put into practice?

The pressure of ideals
Ordinary people – especially women – were offered an ideal of behaviour prescribed by Church and clerical authority. Chaucer shows it at work in the *Tales* through the stories of such figures as the Pardoner, the Parson, the Friar, the Second Nun and the Wife herself.

This authority was further institutionalised in a wealth of treatises and literatures – poems; stories; saints' lives; theological, medical and philosophical tracts; the Bible – and taught via the pulpit and other offices of the Church.

It is an authority, too, that was largely disseminated by men, by male clerics and writers, and supported – as we have just seen the Parson do – by reference to earlier works. Written knowledge, in particular, thus became sacrosanct, the standard by which all else should be judged. Chaucer is, therefore, part of that process.

Authorising marriage

The opening to *The Merchant's Tale* raises the question of the purpose of marriage when a sixty-year-old bachelor decides it is time he wed.

Januarie offers a range of reasons supporting his decision. Marriage, he says, is a 'hooly boond' (IV(E), 1261) and a wife the best part of man's 'tresor' (1270). He determines to choose a young woman on whom he might beget an heir (1270–72). Januarie looks forward to a 'buxom' [obedient] wife (1287), one true and eager to care for him, to love and serve him till death (1286–92). Anticipating the joys of the 'yok of mariage' (1285), he asserts that a wife is 'Goddes yifte' (1311) and marriage 'a ful greet sacrement' (1319). The union is of 'O flessh' (1335) with woman subservient to man. This is why, he reasons, God created Eve – to be 'mannes helpe and his confort' (1324–31). She is made to help him work, keep house and do exactly as he requires with no contradiction (1338–46).

Januarie is repeating what we already know from our earlier explorations. What is important though is that he convinces himself of the righteousness of marriage by quoting a range of authorities to justify his belief:

1. He cites Rebecca, Judith, Abigail and Esther as examples of women's good advice (1366–74).

2. In addition, he notes Seneca's praise of a humble wife as being 'superlatyf' in all virtues, plus Cato's command to endure women's exhortations (1375–77).

3. The ultimate precedent – Christian – is offered in 'Love wel thy wyf, as Crist loved his chirche' (1384).

A diversity of views

What Chaucer offers is also a diversity of views through other tales and other characters. The narrator of *The Merchant's Tale* begins his story with a lament about the woes of marriage, a sacrament that has brought him personally only 'sorwe and care' (IV(E), 1228), 'wepyng and waylyng' (1213). He describes his own wife as the worst (1218) and swears that were she wed to the devil himself she would outdo him (1219–20). Her malice is unspeakable according to the Merchant for she is a 'shrewe'. If he had his time again, he would never 'comen in the snare' (1221–27). He claims he could never begin to catalogue the pain of his wife's 'cursednesse' (1233–39). In fact, he has been married only two months.

This complaint strikes a chord with Harry Bailly who, on several occasions, reveals his bitterness as a married man, as we saw in the opening chapter. Chaucer is able to employ these interludes in the dramatic frame to open up an ongoing debate. The subject itself – marriage – is, ostensibly, its focus. But the underlying theme is the question of knowledge and authority.

When Januarie cites a wealth of biblical and written precedents on the joys of marriage, his words match the institutionalisation of such authority seen in *The Parson's Tale*. Presumably Januarie's knowledge stems from reading and listening to clerical teaching. It does not come from personal experience, unlike that of Harry or the Merchant.

▶ *Key point* – Chaucer is highlighting a potential clash between written, clerical authority and everyday experience, a gap between the ideal (how we *ought* to live our lives) and ordinary practice (how we *do* live our lives).

Everyday experience

The Miller's Tale

This conflict between bookish authority and everyday experience is exemplified in *The Miller's Tale*. Its opening depicts Nicholas, a poor young student studying the Arts at university. His real interest lies in astrology about which he has a smattering of knowledge (I(A), 3190–98). Nicholas lodges in the home of John the carpenter, recently married to a young woman. His room there is filled with books, with his 'Almageste' (a treatise on astrology) and his astrolabe (3208–09). Anxious to consummate an affair with John's new bride, Nicholas concocts an elaborate plan to enable them to spend the night together.

Fearing another Noah's flood and desperate to save his beloved Alison, John agrees to Nicholas's demand that he build three separate boats, one for each, and hang them from the rafters in the roof. John's credulous gullibility is deepened by two things. The first is Nicholas's citation of authorities 'proving' his warning of a second flood. Claiming to know of 'Cristes conseil', he swears John to silence for fear of divine vengeance (3504–07). Nicholas offers a saying by Solomon in general support of good advice. He also reminds John that Noah was only saved because God warned him (3526–35). In order to save Alison, John must, therefore, do as he says.

As he elaborates the plan, Nicholas twice insists on the need for absolute silence. On each occasion, this is reinforced by biblical authority. It is, he says, 'Goddes owene heeste [commandment] deere' (3588) and adds that he cannot explain it for 'I wol nat tellen Goddes pryvetee' (3558). Nicholas's superior knowledge is, thus, vested in Christian authority. In addition, he suggests to John that Noah always wanted to keep *his* wife safe in a separate ark. In this way, he takes advantage of John's ignorance and emotional attachment to Alison, as well as ensuring he separates him from her (3538–46).

The second aspect of the plan is witnessed at the start of the proceedings. Pretending to be in a trance, Nicholas refuses to leave his room. A worried John sends his servant to check on him. John fears that something is badly amiss for today he saw a body being carried into church. On the previous Monday he had seen with his own eyes that same man alive and at his work (3425–30).

John is convinced of his premonition when the servant reports that Nicholas is sitting bolt upright in bed as if moon-struck. This, says John, is what happens to a man who meddles in astronomy. He argues that men should not seek to know of God's secrets and cites the example of a clerk's obsession with astronomy. The clerk walks the fields 'for to prye' upon the stars. He is so busy looking up to heaven that he fails to see the clay pit into which he subsequently falls (3457–61).

Conclusion

What this entertaining interlude highlights is not purely John's simple ignorance but a clash between authority and experience. John relies upon what he can actually see with his own eyes as evidence of authority and truth. He witnesses a man drop dead – a premonition of disaster – plus a crazed Nicholas entranced in his bed and a man fall into a pit – proof of the dangers of studying. What he cannot literally see – God's secrets – he thinks we should not meddle in.

For John, faith is blindly superstitious. He cites biblical authority only as a curse: 'by Seint Thomas' (3425/3461) and 'Help us, Seinte Frydeswyde!' (3449). Later, he calls on Christ and St Benedict to bless Nicholas's room (3483). Christian faith and superstitious belief mingle as he urges Nicholas to awake and think on Christ's Passion. At the same time, he makes the sign of the cross above him and at each corner of the room while chanting a charm against evil spirits (3477–86). So, when Nicholas claims to have seen Christ's plan for a flood upon the Earth, John is fooled. His citation of Christian authority frightens John and ensures his belief.

The problem of knowledge

Here Chaucer calls into question the nature of knowledge. In what can we trust?

1. Our experience?
2. Our faith in the unseen, in God?
3. Do we accept the evidence of our own eyes, or what others – books, clerics, the Church – tell us?

These are the problems to which we are returned time and again.

A struggle for power

The Wife of Bath's fight with her beloved fifth husband, the clerk Jankyn, is born of a frustrated desire to confront an authoritative tradition that rejects women as inferior and dangerous beings. At first glance, their struggle appears to return us to a notion of 'maistrie' idealised in *The Franklin's Tale*.

She tells us that he beats her (III(D), 505–07/511), blows she will feel on her ribs as long as she lives. Yet, she loves him best of all (512–13). Once, he punched her on the ear leaving her deaf (634–40), but, in return, she refuses to be silent or kept in . When she describes their battle, it ends with her insistence that 'He yaf me al the bridel in myn hond' (813). In the end, she achieves domination over him for he gave her 'al the soveraynetee' (818).

What is the precise nature of this fight? When they are first married, Alison continues her gallivanting despite Jankyn's constant repetition of proverbs and stories to prevent her (641–61). What angers her is his insistence upon reading a particular book he calls 'Valerie and Theofraste' (671). This is a collection of antifeminist tracts by writers such as Valerius, Theophrastus, St. Jerome, Tertullian and a host of others (671–81), all bound in one volume. Reading it is Jankyn's favourite occupation. As a result, Alison claims he knows more about wicked wives than he does good ones (682–87).

Their battle commences when Alison rips out three pages of his book and punches him in the face (788–93). Her action is symbolic of a declared war of the sexes and an attempt for a woman to make her voice heard. Her provocation, though, has been intense. Jankyn reads and then repeats an array of tales: of Eve taking the apple so that woman is the 'los of al mankynde' (720); of treacherous women like Delilah, Amphiorax, Livia and Lucia; of cruel and lecherous women such as Clytemnestra or the Queen of Crete.

Jankyn tells, too, of wives who slay their husbands as they sleep so that they can enjoy their lovers or, simply, those who berate them as in the example of Socrates whose wife 'caste pisse upon his heed' (713–71). Finally, he cites numerous proverbs about women's nagging, anger and voracious lust (773–85).

This is the background against which the entire *Prologue* is set. As fast as Chaucer proposes the Wife as an example of a potential rebel (albeit a humorous one), he simultaneously reminds us of the very rules against which she is judged and found wanting. In spite of this ambiguity, when Alison asks us who could ever guess 'the wo that in my herte was, and peyne?', its poignancy reverberates throughout the tale. (787) When she assaults her husband, she strikes a blow against his authority – not simply against his traditional domination in marriage, but what he and his books represent.

Jankyn is a cleric, one who teaches others. His own learning is founded in both the institution of the Church – which he represents – and an entire heritage of written works. What he repeats is, therefore, powerful and authoritative. Alison is offered a gold standard for wifely behaviour and fails to measure up. So, when she tears up his book and hits him, her actions directly challenge an authoritative tradition that damns her whether she behaves correctly or not. As a woman, a daughter of Eve, she is herself the bringer of pain to women *and* men, as our earlier reference showed. Thus, Chaucer uses the *Wife of Bath's Prologue* to open up some fundamental questions.

A material evidence

A similar authorial strategy is witnessed in *The Pardoner's Prologue*. As an official representative of the Church, the Pardoner is invested with a special authority. In return for money, he will grant forgiveness for sins. He preaches to ordinary people in an effort to encourage them to donate to Church coffers. In his description of how he does this, we see, once again, that division of authority opened up in *The Miller's Tale*.

The Pardoner's flock are clearly, like John the carpenter, simple people who mix Christian faith and superstitious belief. What they trust is John's material world, things they can see and touch. The Pardoner, thus, begins by showing them his indulgences or papal bulls and the 'lordes seel on my patente'. He claims that this protects him and allows him to proceed, unhindered, with God's work. What he offers is visual evidence of the authority vested in him by the Church (VI(C), 335–40).

It is seen, too, in his array of relics, glass cases full of rags and bones, all designed to confirm faith and support Christian 'truth'. For each, the Pardoner invents a story. This, he says, is the shoulder bone of a holy Jew's sheep. Washed in any well, it protects from disease all animals that drink there. Or, used in a soup, it heals the jealous heart (347–71). He shows them a mitten, too, one that 'ye may se' or touch. Anyone placing a hand in it will ensure the multiplication of his grain (372–74).

A tangible authority

The Pardoner's authority is, then, a tangible one. It is supported by his eloquent teaching, sermons on how money is the root of all evil, holy stories and a few words in Latin, certain to impress (333–34/341–45). He encourages everyone to confess even the smallest sin. Those who do can be absolved – for a price – 'by the auctoritee/Which that by bulle ygraunted was to me' (387–88). In this way, the power of both the Church and the written word is confirmed.

That all is a trick is something we explore in the next chapter.

Tutorial

Further reading

Examine the argument between Chauntecleer and Pertelote on the nature of dreams in *The Nun's Priest's Tale*. Read the reasoned debate of *The Tale of Melibee*. Look at Dorigen's consideration of 'auctoritee' that seems to advise her suicide in *The Franklin's Tale*.

Progress questions

1. Describe some of the medieval ideals that Chaucer presents us with.

2. How does Chaucer undercut those ideals? Refer in detail to at least 2 tales.

3. How and why does Chaucer present a clash between authority and experience?

Knowledge and Experience

Study tips

1. Once you've read some critical material, write a two or three line summary on the views of each critic.

2. Approach critical works as you would literature. Interrogate the text by examining language and vocabulary used. Look at the logical progression of their argument and try to identify any flaws or weaknesses. Ask yourself if their argument is supported by reference to the text(s).

3. After your reading, take a break. Go away and sort out your own ideas and opinions. See where you agree with or differ from the critics. Note your reasons.

Assignment topics

1. Consider the ways in which the texts you have read invite multiple interpretations.

2. Consider Chaucer's treatment and presentation of *one* of the following: marriage; women; religion.

3. How far might Chaucer be said to fracture the notion and/or the need for authority in his writing?

9

Fracturing Authority

One-minute summary – Chaucer challenges masculine authority by offering his own interpretation of it. He asserts the ambiguous and contradictory nature of authority, thereby subjecting it to question. He opens up a gap between an abstract ideal and its application to everyday life. Chaucer elides closure and definitive answers. In this chapter we will explore:

- raising possibilities
- personal interpretation
- the authority debate
- debunking the myth
- subverting and rejecting
- care of the soul
- a perfect exchange
- eliding closure

Raising possibilities

The Pardoner asserts both religious and political (Church) as well as written authority. Other aspects of his *Prologue* complicate this view, however, and point towards the possibility that Chaucer uses this speaker to question the nature of this authority.

His choice of the word 'gaude' [trick], as he tells how his skill has won him a hundred marks a year, alerts us to a crucial element of the Pardoner's preaching ((VI(C), 389). He tells 'an hundred false japes moore' (394), tricking his audience into parting with money. One of his most astonishing admissions is that though the theme of his sermon is always avarice, it is a vice of which he himself 'be gilty' (428–29). Thus, the Pardoner's rhetoric and eloquence is designed purely for financial gain.

He confesses that he cares nothing 'for correccioun of synne' or whether their 'soules goon a-blakeberyed!' (398–406). It is clear that the Pardoner despises his ignorant and gullible audience who are easily fooled by fake relics and clever teaching of 'ensamples' and 'olde stories' (435–38). In other words, the religious authority upon which he bases his work is, by his own admission, worthless.

What is Chaucer doing here? Is the Pardoner an aberration, do you think, a misfit? Or, is he intended to be typical of his profession, so that Chaucer's depiction of him is an attack upon the practice of pardoning rather than upon the character? Is the author a radical, challenging the very authority of the Church whose influence was all-pervasive? Or, is he simply asking questions of this powerful institution to remind us that it is not infallible?

The Wife of Bath
In a similar way, the *Wife of Bath's Prologue* opens by raising a series of questions about the undisputed authority not only of Church teaching but of the written word itself. Alison begins by commenting upon the technique of 'glosyng' where male clerics and other writers offer commentaries upon and interpretations of the Bible. It is a process that leads to definitive statements about Christ's intentions or meaning. This, in turn, permits the establishment of ideals governing belief and behaviour, some of which we studied earlier. Thus, Alison's remarks bring into sharp focus some fundamental tenets of medieval life.

Personal interpretation

In part, Alison's opening speech about the desirability of chastity and the purpose of marriage is an attempt to justify her own life.

1. She cites the examples of Solomon, Abraham and Jacob as proof that there is nothing inherently sinful in multiple marriages (III(D), 55–57/35–43).

2. Equally, she refers to the single recorded instance of Christ's attendance at a wedding as actually failing to provide clear example that she should only have wed once (9–13).

3. Christ's reproof to the Samaritan – who, like Alison, had five husbands – equally lacks clarity. When He says that she was not properly married, the Wife argues that we 'kan nat seyn' what was meant (20).

Thus, Alison's remark that though men may conjecture and 'glose', no-one can ever finally say what is true, highlights another aspect of this interlude. What she asserts is ambiguity rather than the definitive proof which authority was intended to provide. If the Bible provides written evidence, then it is, according to Alison, contradictory. It tells us 'to wexe and multiplye' (28), to leave our mothers and marry, 'But of no nombre mencion made he' (32). There are gaps in a written tradition that demand interpretation – hence, the practice of 'glosyng'. Yet that same practice can never finally agree *because* of those gaps.

▶ *Key point* – For Alison such ambiguity means that she can rebel against men's supposedly final 'truths' and provide her own alternative version, which is precisely what she does.

Her reading of St. Paul's comment on the exemplarity of virginity is that it was not a commandment. The Wife finds contradictory evidence for, equally, he advised that it was better to marry than to burn, while Christ never ordered chastity either. Without marriage, she argues, we could not legitimately reproduce. She concludes that virginity is merely a choice, one not attainable to all. Instead, she prefers to 'bistowe the flour of al myn age/In the actes and in fruyt of mariage' (60–113).

Using lived experience to challenge authority

This challenges written and clerical authority. Alison inverts the usual process of defining authority by taking her lived experience and 'matching' it against a citation – rather than using the ideal, the citation, as an example of how to live.

So, she asks where did God forbid marriage: 'By expres word? I pray yow, telleth me' (61). By her reasoning, what is written is open to interpretation and, therefore, unreliable. Instead, she offers knowledge of 'Experience' rather than 'auctoritee' (1). Her perception of ordinary living means that 'herde I nevere tellen in myn age' (24) a limit upon the number of marriage partners she might take. Her whole life, since the age of twelve, has been devoted to marriage (4). This, she implies, – in an echo of the Clerk's explication of the lesson of his story – is how most people live, not according to exemplary and unattainable ideals.

A confrontation – unresolved

Again, we witness a confrontation between knowledge gained from experience and abstract, bookish authority, one that Chaucer does not – indeed, perhaps cannot – finally resolve.

Nevertheless, by asking his audience to consider it, he raises the possibility of a critique of the very structure of his society. His challenge is to notions of fixed authority. Here he offers us Alison's personal and unique view. Through it, he is able to disrupt that notion and suggest it is far more slippery than many of his age might have accepted.

The authority debate

Authority of experience is what the god Pluto seems to confirm towards the end of *The Merchant's Tale*, as he and Proserpine observe May's treachery in Januarie's walled garden. It is experience, Pluto reasons, that daily proves the many treasons done to man by women.

Yet, the examples he cites as evidence are taken not from life but from 'Ten hondred thousand [tales]' (IV(E), 2237–41). His authorities are the words of Solomon who can find no praiseworthy women, or Jesus Syrak, author of *Ecclesiastus* (2242–75). The visual evidence of May's planned trickery of blind Januarie confirms Pluto's reading, as, suddenly, knowledge (from books *and* life) comes together. Thus, he swears to grant Januarie the return of his sight so that he can have material proof of her wickedness (2251–63).

The situation is made more complex, however, by Proserpine's challenge to her consort. She argues that women's boldness enables them to face down and contradict all that men see with their eyes (2264–75). She implies that since men say women are 'jangleresses' [chatterboxes] (2307), they might as well live up to it and use verbal dexterity to outwit men. This is the gift that she, in her turn, grants to May (2305-09).

In addition, she refutes Pluto's knowledge by dismissing the authorities he relies upon. Solomon, she says, was a lecherous fool who worshipped false idols and was only spared divine retribution for his father's sake. Proof is only 'as seith the book' (2300). Equally, Pluto's stories tell of women 'ful trewe, ful goode, and vertuous' (2281), a fact confirmed, too, in Roman 'geestes' [histories] (2284). The ultimate authority – the Bible – suggests that perfection can only be found in God alone and not in men *or* women. Hence, Proserpine refers to the 'sentence of the man' (2288). Consequently, she asks, why should she care for 'youre auctoritees?' (2277). Instead, she rejects entirely the villainy written about women. In short, it is not worth 'a boterflye!' (2304).

Once again, this quarrel opens up a series of questions about the reliability of traditionally authoritative sources. Written authority becomes a matter of interpreting a range of references that may be ambiguous or contradictory. Experiential knowledge (what you know or see from life) is, interestingly, no more reliable – just as the Pardoner's tangible relics were fake.

It seems then, that a single definitive answer is found only in 'verray God that nys but oon' (2291). How to arrive at that final truth remains unclear. Despite the evidence of his own eyes, Januarie is deceived by May's glossing of her behaviour. Januarie claims he *saw* that Damyan 'swyved thee' (2378). May insists that he saw imperfectly for his suddenly returned sight will need time to adjust (3295-2406). Crucially it is 'glosyng' or interpretation that wins the day and denies all facts.

Here Chaucer undermines the very notion of authority by drawing our attention to what it conceals or (deliberately?) misreads. Though softened by the humour of this tale, the effects of such a notion are potentially radical. If the only true authority is God, then all other standards are subject to a continual process of interpretation. In this way everyday authority can only ever be contradictory and ambiguous.

Debunking the myth

The Pardoner's Tale confirms this idea. As we have seen, the Pardoner is well-practised in deception. He knows the methods of his trade 'by rote' (VI(C), 332). His tongue is quick. In churches across the land he adopts 'an hauteyn speche' that rings out as 'round as gooth a belle' (330–31). One of his special tricks is to single out a member of his audience and 'stynge hym with my tonge smerte' (413). He castigates this person from the pulpit, denouncing them as sinful and, without actually naming them, signalling their identity to his audience. Even he admits that this is a vindictive act (412–22).

The Pardoner follows this frank admission of his trickery with a sermon on his usual theme, the evil of money. At its conclusion, he calls upon the assembled company to offer to his relics and receive pardon for their sins (926). In addition he reminds them that they might seek absolution any time throughout the pilgrimage to Canterbury for they are fortunate in having a pardoner (him) in their fellowship (919–40). He then urges Harry Bailly 'Ye for a grote! Unbokele anon thy purs' (945).

The Pardoner chooses Harry for he is 'moost envoluped in synne' (942). What makes this remark so shocking is the nature of the Pardoner's previous confession. It may well be that the sins of the three rioters of his sermon – swearing, drinking and gambling – apply to Harry. But the Pardoner himself is also guilty of them. Here we see his flagrant contempt for the stupidity of his audience. His fellow pilgrims already know how he cons them for he has already related the tricks of his trade *and* his own disregard for the welfare of their souls.

Not surprisingly, the Pardoner's shameless dismissal of his own occupation elicits a strong response from the Host, as we saw in chapter 1. Harry's foul-mouthed attack on the Pardoner's dubious masculinity is part of his own inner fears. Yet his language also reveals a fierce repudiation of the authority vested in the office of any pardoner. His reaction to being singled out challenges and debunks the authority of both the man and his role.

Let us remind ourselves of what the Host says. He claims that the Pardoner would have him kiss his old underpants and swear it was the relic of a saint. For his part, he would rather have the Pardoner's 'coillons' in his hand than any relic or sanctuary [a box of relics] so that he, in cruel parody of a pardoner, might carry them around with him enshrined in 'an hogges toord!' (949–55).

Spiritual authority belied by coarseness
Harry's coarse terminology suggests a basic refutation of the abstract, spiritual authority with which the job of a pardoner is, supposedly, permeated. As such it shatters all claims to power the Pardoner might care to make. Though, as we saw earlier, the Pardoner attempts to appeal to the visual, material and everyday experience of his 'parishioners', his intent is radically undermined by his own admissions. He shows them his official documents as proof of his authority. He shows them, too, his sheep's bone and other relics that he subsequently reveals are fake. He admits that he cares only for personal, financial reward and nothing for anyone's soul. Why then should Harry – or anyone else – believe anything he says or does?

As the Host remarks, the Pardoner would attempt to pass off his own stained underpants and have us trust in its spiritual value. Harry's language juxtaposes the body (dirty pants, testicles, pig's excrement, his own hand) with the soul. Instead of accepting the soul as authority, by virtue of its spiritual and superior status, he declares his faith in the body. In other words, Harry's words elevate human experience, everyday knowledge, that which he *knows*. The Pardoner's authority – the Christian Word his office mediates – is vague and abstract. Even worse, he admits himself that it is not to be trusted.

What Chaucer demonstrates through the fictional voice of the Pardoner is that, once again, any ideal or definitive authority is potentially flawed or ambiguous. The Pardoner's response to Harry is silence; there is no reply to this direct challenge to the authority of the Church. That is not to say that Chaucer is rebelling against a final 'truth', that of God Himself. But what is clear is his dislike of the abuse and manipulation of that ultimate authority, one that takes place through the corrupt agency of some of its official representatives.

Subverting and rejecting

We see this, too, in *The Summoner's Tale*. The Summoner and the Friar are deadly rivals in the dramatic frame of the *Tales*, though both are officers of the Church. The Summoner's rejection of any moral or spiritual authority vested in the Friar is seen in the *Prologue* to his tale. He relates how a friar is given a vision of hell in which Satan lifts up his huge tail to 'Shewe forth thyn ers'. Nesting within is a mass of friars (III(D), 1675–99). Again, a spiritual office is equated with the filth and sin of the body. The authority of the Friar, and, by implication, the office that he represents is, thus, derided.

This is replicated in *The Summoner's Tale* itself. It is told, in part, to gain revenge on the previous story by the Friar. Like pardoners, friars relied upon their verbal eloquence in preaching. The Summoner, then, tells of a 'lymtour' [friar] travelling around and preaching in a small church in Yorkshire. There he calls upon his audience to consider the value of 'trentals' whereby thirty requiem masses are sung in order to expedite a soul's journey to heaven (1709–28).

The friar's occupation, like the Pardoner's, is intended for the welfare of souls. In return for money, the singing of a mass will deliver them from pain (1741). The friar emphasises the difficulty of doing this, thereby stressing the importance of his own role (1729–32). The spiritual intent of the friar's purpose, however, is undercut by the narrator's careful recording of his intended financial gain.

At the start, he notes how the friar begged people to give money 'for Goddes sake' in order to speed the building of churches. Don't offer it, the friar says, to 'possessioners', those clergy or laymen in receipt of endowments to support them. They, thanks to God, live in 'wele and habundaunce' (1715–23). He implies that friars are poor in comparison and rely on begging to live. This is what we see him do.

He and his colleague first collect from the pulpit and then go door to door asking for 'mele and chese, or elles corn'. One of them writes down the names of all who donate 'Ascaunces [as if] that he wolde for hem preye'. Together they call on folk to give them food or goods in kind, or else money (1735–53). Once again, visual proof of the authority of these men is important. The friar bears with him the outward symbols of his power, his 'scrippe [satchel] and tipped staf' (1737). His companion has a folding set of writing tables and a stylus with which he notes the names of the generous.

This is, apparently, a tangible exchange. The people see 'lo! Heere I write youre/name –', veritable evidence of the spiritual penance they buy. In addition, the items carried by the friars give them their air of authority. Yet we are offered proof of the suspect nature of that authority when the Summoner tells us that as soon as they are out of the door their servant 'planed awey the names everichon' that have been inscribed on the tables. In this way, the friar is said to serve them 'with nyfles [trifles] and with fables [lies]' (1754–60).

This remark causes a storm of protest with an interruption from the Friar himself, one over-ridden by Harry Bailly who urges the Summoner to spare no details. The credibility of friars, already seriously damaged, is further destroyed as the Summoner tells of the contrast between the inner and outer man.

Eventually the friar in the Summoner's story arrives at the house of bedridden Thomas where he proceeds to make himself at home. He shoos away the pet cat, lays down his bag and staff, and settles on the bench (1770–80). Later, he steals a cheeky kiss from Thomas's wife. He flirts with her and declares her the prettiest he has seen all day (1801–09). He eagerly accepts her invitation to dine yet insists that he is a man who eats little, for his nourishment is spiritual. His body, he claims, is wasted by suffering. Yet he drools over the possibility of eating chicken livers and roast pork (1838–47). Thus, this friar is a hypocrite, a liar, a glutton in search of the good life and material gain.

Care of the soul?

The friar speaks at length throughout the tale to explicate his role and stress its spiritual nature. He boasts of emulating the disciples by being a skilful preacher and a fisher of men's souls; unlike lazy curates, to spread the word of Christ is 'set al myn entente' (1816–22). His repeated use of the pronoun 'we' – 'we mendynantz [mendicants], we freres' for example (1912) – ostensibly establishes him as part of a spiritual and authoritative sect. He claims to live in poverty, abstinence, charity and humility and to despise worldly trappings (1873–1917), though we know this is untrue. In citing biblical ideals he attempts to align himself with the ultimate authority, Christ. Yet this external show fails to match inner virtue.

The friar's audacity knows no bounds. Seizing the opportunity to extract money from the family, he agrees to shrive [cleanse] Thomas of his sins, at the request of his wife. He begins to preach at length at Thomas's bedside. The friar has a saying and an authority to support it for every occasion. Earlier, having greedily accepted the invitation to dine, he cited the exemplary abstinence of Moses, the prophet Elijah and Christ who 'as hooly wit devyseth,/Yaf us ensample of fastynge and preyeres' (1904–05). He relates a long-winded story from Seneca as a warning against the sin of anger (2017–41) plus a host of other examples and mottos ranging from the King of Persia to the 'Placebo' of Psalm 114:9 (2043–85).

The friar begs for Thomas's help – in other words, money – with yet another appeal to Christian authority and the charity of 'oure Lord!' (2107–20). Though Thomas insists that he has already confessed today (2094–95), the friar continues his verbal onslaught. His repeated reference to divine authority and the example of Jesus is, then, designed to extort money and to enhance his own false credibility.

The Summoner records the friar's fictitious claim that he needs Thomas's gold for the building of a church. He claims to owe forty pounds for stones (2106) and warns that he and his fellows risk having to sell their books to raise the cash. Without them, he asks, how might we preach and so save the world (2103–20)? Here we see how the spiritual nature of books is abased.

A perfect exchange

Like the Pardoner, this friar relies upon both the outward symbols of his power (his bag and staff) and his eloquence. Friars – and priests – base their preaching upon the 'glosyng' or interpretation of the Bible and other written authorities. Their words derive an authority of their own from such a source. Yet, as we have seen, the friar is a liar, his preaching full of hot air. His words are a blatant abuse of his position and so receive a highly entertaining reply.

Thomas's everyday experience informs him that some of those in the office of the Church are not to be trusted, despite their inflated claims. He tells the friar that he has a little something for him and his brethren. He invites him to slide his hand down his back and feel around for his gift. There, he says, beneath 'my buttok' is something 'I have hyd in pryvetee' (2129–43). The friar duly gropes 'Aboute his tuwel' until suddenly Thomas 'leet the frere a fart', one louder than a horse (2145–51). Thus, the empty, hollow sound of the friar's preaching is rewarded with the same.

This exchange should have been a spiritual one, authoritative learning given in return for a donation to the church building scheme. Yet, in reality, it is base, and thoroughly material. The friar offers empty rhetoric to what he perceives as a gullible old fool. His demand is for gold, a gift he finds hidden in the cleft of Thomas's buttocks. The import of the friar's words is negligible, just a 'fart' dispersed on the air, a literal blast of contempt that shatters all pretensions to spiritual authority.

▶ *Key point* – Chaucer uses the comedy of this tale to critique the corruption of the Church, or, at least, some of its agents. Equally, he is able to subvert the authority of an entire tradition of teaching and learning. The written word – in the shape of the Bible or other books or examples – is invested with a special power. This is subsequently translated by clerics and scholars and used to set up an ideal of behaviour, as we have already seen. When the friar does it, his words are false. Thomas's common sense tells him this. Elevated rhetoric masquerading as the welfare of souls counts for nothing in the physical expulsion of air from the body.

Eliding closure

The Summoner's Tale returns us, then, to some crucial questions. In what might we trust? What exactly is Chaucer's intent? Does he attempt to offer us definitive answers or merely open up perspectives and multiply possibility?

Chaucer has presented us with two sets of oppositions:

1. spirituality – the welfare of souls, plus biblical and clerical words and precedents, *versus* physicality – the body, its excrement, its flatulence, its anus and testicles)

2. knowledge (the written, the clerical word) *versus* experience (everyday life).

In each, the first of these, in theory at least, is invested with authority. Yet, as we have seen, the other half of these polarities consistently calls into question the very nature of that authority. As fast as one asserts itself, Chaucer works to undo it.

However, most of our examples are comic tales, or else, as in the case of the dominant fictitious voices of the Pardoner and the Wife of Bath, are 'problem' poems. To what extent might Chaucer's apparent attack upon the institutions of his day lack serious intent?

Humour with criticism

It may well be that humour allows Chaucer to soften and distance his criticism. We are not given biting satire but, instead, are invited to consider these notions more deeply, to face up to their inherent ambiguities. Such ambivalence does not detract from its impact. Instead it challenges us to read beyond surface appearance.

Some of the tales of the last two chapters *are* serious, a factor that ought to alert us to the over-arching significance of the ideas explored. Others, though humorous, may also have a darker vein. The Wife of Bath presents her own 'glosyng' of written authority. She offers, too, the example of her personal experience warning that 'I shal telle ensamples mo than ten' (III(D), 179). She may well typify every feature of woman so feared by the antifeminist tracts Jankyn reads, but Chaucer cleverly persuades us of her 'human' individuality. When, for example, she poignantly cries 'But – Lord Crist! – whan that it remem-/breth me/Upon my youthe, and on my jolitee,/It tikleth me aboute myn herte roote' (469–71), we are invited to forget that she is constructed through her 'own' narrative.

At the same time she remarks that it is impossible for clerks to speak well of women unless they refer to their ideals of saints' lives. She suggests that there are alternatives. If women had written works like men, 'they wolde han writen of men moore wikkednesse/Than al the mark of Adam may redresse' (693–96). Only one story has been heard. Women's enforced silence ensures their subordination through the complex workings of a powerful institution whose authority is based upon a partial and selective tradition of storytelling.

Alison asks 'Who peyntede the leon, tel me who?' (688–92). Here she refers to the lion's question upon seeing a picture of a man killing a lion. Her words are not simply the idiosyncratic response of a particularised individual. Instead, through her voice, Chaucer calls attention to the abstract nature of an authority that can only offer examples far removed from the lives of ordinary people. Where, asks the Wife, am *I* in your books? What possible impact, asks Chaucer, can such empty rhetoric and idealised notions have upon men and women?

The Wife's answer is simply that women might one day respond in kind. One reading of her *Prologue* and *Tale* emphasises a war of the sexes. Yet neither the inversion of power nor its cancellation through the notion of equality is enough. Chaucer shows us through the example of the Wife of Bath how opinions are formed by listening to the authoritative and idealised comments of others *and* on the basis of practical, lived experience.

Alison demands to know why her perspective is any less powerful or 'correct' than any other. Her beliefs are juxtaposed with those of others in the *Tales*: the Franklin's idealistic vision of equality; the Pardoner's self-confessed abuse of an authority he relies upon for financial reward; John the carpenter's faith in the tangible world he inhabits as ultimate proof of knowledge; and so on. Each elides definition and a single interpretation.

Conclusion

The Canterbury Tales offers us an array of tales, genres, storytellers and narrative levels. Myriad voices and a host of shifting perspectives clamour and clash in this lengthy, unfinished collection. In it, Chaucer confronts the very notion of writing itself.

▶ *Key point* – What Chaucer offers, finally, is his own challenge to received notions of authority and to any evidence that the written word might remain fixed as 'truth'. Instead, all is open to question, is multiple and, finally, ambiguous.

Review of section

In this section we have seen how:

1. the nature of knowledge is open and shifting with a contrast between the abstract (books, clerical and Church teaching) and lived, everyday experience/ the material and the tangible

2. all writing and the ideals inscribed in it are subject to a process of interpretation that raises the question: whose is the definitive viewpoint?

3. Chaucer's work is resistant to definition and his writings open and multiple.

Tutorial

Further reading
Read *The Tale of Melibee* and *The Nun's Priest's Tale*. See if you can apply some of the ideas offered in this chapter to those texts.

Discussion points
1. Why does Chaucer refuse to offer us final answers or definitions?

2. What is Chaucer up to when he offsets everyday experience against the ideal? Which, if any, do you think he finally believes in?

3. Is the only or ultimate authority in the *Tales* that of God?

Assignment tips
1. Re-read your notes after tutorials and follow areas of concern and/or interest.

2. Try to narrow down an essay topic so that you distil the main areas in a wide question.

3. Remember to analyse and argue rather than describe in essays: focus on the *why* and *how* rather than the *what*.

Assignment topics
1. Chaucer is firmly on the side of masculine authority. Do you agree?

2. Chaucer's concern is with the gulf between the secular and the spiritual, the ideal and its practice rather than any possible mediation between the two. How far do you agree with this statement?

3. Chaucer is a subversive and a radical writer. His poems challenge some fundamental notions of medieval existence. Discuss.

Wider Reading

Use some of the ideas in this study as a framework for your own exploration of some of Chaucer's other work. Try reading *The Legend of Good Women*, *The Parliament of Fowls*, *The Book of the Duchess*, *The House of Fame* or *Troilus and Criseyde*.

You also need to familiarise yourself with the work of the critics. The following is a select bibliography only. Use your university or college's on-line library system to help you find more. There are also several excellent periodicals largely devoted to Chaucer: *The Chaucer Review*, *Studies in the Age of Chaucer* and *The Chaucer Yearbook*.

General introductions

Gail Ashton, *Chaucer, 'The Canterbury Tales'* (Macmillan, 1998). Detailed analysis of some tales plus commentary on several influential critics.

D. S. Brewer, *A New Introduction to Chaucer* (Longman, 1998). A useful all-rounder

Steve Ellis, *Geoffrey Chaucer* (Northcote House, 1996) – a short but excellent critical study.

Feminist approaches or those informed by gender

Catherine S. Cox, *Gender and Language in Chaucer* (University Press of Florida, 1997).

Sheila Delany, *Writing Woman: Women Writers and Women in Literature, Medieval to Modern* (Schoken Books, 1983) and *Medieval Literary Politics* (Manchester University Press, 1990).

Carolyn Dinshaw, *Chaucer's Sexual Poetics* (University of Wisconsin Press, 1989).

Elaine Tuttle Hansen, *Chaucer and the Fictions of Gender* (University of California Press, 1992).
Anne Laskaya, *Chaucer's Approach to Gender in 'The Canterbury Tales'* (Boydell and Brewer, 1995).
Jill Mann, *Geoffrey Chaucer* (Harvester Wheatsheaf, 1991).
Priscilla Martin, *Chaucer's Women: Nuns, Wives and Amazons* (Macmillan, 1990).

Others

David Aers, *Chaucer* (Harvester Press, 1986). An interesting, New Historicist approach that places Chaucer in his medieval context.
Helen Cooper, *The Structure of 'The Canterbury Tales'* (Duckworth, 1983). Considers genre, story and the intertextuality of the *Tales*.
Alfred David, *The Strumpet Muse* (Indiana University Press, 1976). Still a useful humanist approach that considers the nature of Chaucer's art.
Steve Ellis, *Chaucer, 'The Canterbury Tales'* (Longman, 1998). An excellent collection of critical essays, all adopting a post-modernist stance.
David Lawton, *Chaucer's Narrators* (Brewer, Chaucer Studies:13, 1985). An exploration of speaker and voice.
Stephen Knight, *Geoffrey Chaucer* (Basil Blackwell, 1986). A Marxist look at the work as social commentary.
V. A. Kolve, *Chaucer and the Imagery of Narrative* (Edward Arnold, 1984). An interesting approach via iconography, structure and patterns of imagery that sees the work as intertextual (several volumes).
Peggy Knapp, *Chaucer and the Social Contest* (Routledge, 1990). Approaches via structure and sees as social critique.
Marion Wynne-Davies ed., *The Tale of the Clerk and the Wife of Bath: Geoffrey Chaucer* (Routledge, 1992). Useful analysis of specific tales.
Paul Strohm, *Social Chaucer* (Harvard University Press, 1989). A New Historicist approach.

Web sites on Chaucer

One-minute summary – The internet, or world wide web, is a useful resource, giving the student nearly free and almost immediate information on any topic. The following list of web sites may be helpful for you. Please note that neither the author nor the publisher is responsible for content or opinions expressed on the sites listed, which are simply intended to offer starting points for students.

Also, please remember that the internet is a fast-evolving environment, and links may come and go. If you have some favourite sites you would like to see mentioned in future editions of this book, please write to Gail Ashton c/o Studymates (address on back cover), or email her at the address shown below. You will find a free selection of useful and readymade student links for Chaucer and many other subjects at the Studymates web site.

Studymates web site: http://www.studymates.co.uk

Gail Ashton email: gailashton@studymates.co.uk

Introduction

You will find a good deal of information about Chaucer and his work on the internet, though, at the moment, web sites tend not to offer scholarly essays. Consequently, your research here is more likely to supplement other reading than to replace it.

Electronic texts

There are many examples of the text of *The Canterbury Tales* online. Most are illustrated while some are interactive with audio-visual aids. Some also offer modern translations. Look at the following:

The Canterbury Tales Project
http://www.shef.ac.uk/uni/projects/ctp/index.html
Offers images and text transcripts. Project Director: Professor N F Blake.

Canterbury Web Site – Chaucer's Canterbury Tales
http://www.cantweb.co.uk/chaucer
See the Albion Bookshop for many Chaucer related books.

Chaucer's Canterbury Tales
http://www.canterburytales.org/canterbury_tales.html
Presented by ELF – welcome to Chaucer's *Canterbury Tales*. An electronic presentation of the classic poem in several editions.

Bonnie Wheeler
http://dcwww.mediasvcs.smu.edu/chaucer
Created by a member of the Southern Methodist University, this supplements text with online research aids.

Geoffrey Chaucer: Canterbury Tales
http://faculty.acu.edu/~appletonl/mb1/ct.htm
Here you can find the complete *Tales* online. The page is produced by a retired Instructor of English at Abilene Christian University.

The Middle English Collection
http://etext.virginia.edu/mideng.browse.html
Contains a variety of texts from Chaucer and his contemporaries in both original and translation. Many illustrated.

The Chaucer Studio
http://www.millersv.edu/~english/homepage/duncan/chaucer/a-udio.html
An audio text with tips on how to read aloud. There are sound clips for Mac or Windows.

Biographical information

Biographical sketches of Memorable Christians of the Past
http://justus.anglican.org/resources/bio/59.html
A biographical outline of Chaucer with hyperlinks running to about 2,800 words.

British Literature
http://www.britishliterature.com/
Use the author search facility to locate information and links on Chaucer.

Encarta
http://encarta.msn.com/
'Your gateway to 16,000 abridged reference articles and our world atlas.' The online encyclopedia from Microsoft.

Encyclopedia.com
http://www.encyclopedia.com/

Librarius
http://www.librarius.com/cantales.htm
Chronology of Geoffrey Chaucer's Life and Times. 'Buy your own copy of *The Canterbury Tales*!' Visit Librarius on-line Bookshop (also for a modern English translation).

Virgil
http://www.virgil.org
Virgil is a source of classical and medieval texts.

Online critical journals/collections of essays

The Chaucer Review
http://www.baylor.edu/~Chaucer-Bibliography
The annotated journal, *The Chaucer Review*.

The New Chaucer Society
http://ncs.rutgers.edu/
A journal and bulletin board for the New Chaucer Society. Offers a forum for teachers and scholars.

Ohio State Press
http://www.ohiostatepress.org/s99/SAC.htm
This contains bibliography, annotations, articles and other critical material on Chaucer as well as volumes of *Studies in the Age of Chaucer*.

Other material

Baragona's Chaucer page
http://www.vmi_edu/~english/chaucer.html
Known as Baragona's Chaucer page, this has bibliographies, a bulletin board, a glossary and the full text of the *Tales*.

The Canon of John Lydgate Project
http://www.ualberta.ca/~sreimer/
Includes a bibliography and course-related material devised by Stephen R. Reimer and John H. Fisher at the University of Alberta.

Chaucer Bibliography
http://www.wsu.ed:8080/~hanly/chaucer/coursematerials/bib.html
A bibliography based on Chaucer and Chaucer studies.

Chaucer in the Library
http://www.smith.edu/libraries/subject/chaucer.htm
This one contains some useful background on history and works, with a bibliography and comments on periodicals and articles. There are helpful web site links. Library references are offered, with a guide to using indexes and MLA to widen searches.

The Chaucer Metapage
http//www.unc.edu/depts/chaucer/index.html
This goes direct to the Chaucer Metapage which contains articles,

ideas and is interactive, welcoming contributions.

Chaucer Outlines
http://geoffreychaucer.org/outlines
Summaries of and study guides to *Troilus* and *The Canterbury Tales*.

Edwin Duncans web pages
http://www.towson.edu/~duncan/chauhom2.html
Here you will find course materials, online research aids and electronic text.

The Ellesmere Text
http://www.jsu.edu/depart/english/treed/chother.htm
The illustrated Ellesmere text with translation and commentaries upon the pilgrims. You will find information on medieval history, biography and links to other sites.

Harvard University
http://icg.harvard.edu/~eng115b/
A source of distance learning page materials.

Luminarium
http://www.luminarium.org/medlit/chauceressay.html
May be useful for essays and articles from both students and critics.

http://www.luminarium.org/medlit/chaucer.htm
Chaucer bibliography, quotes and notes.

http://www.luminarium.org/medlit/chaucer_bib.htm
The page lists Chaucer's works with extra explanations.

http://www.luminarium.org/medlit/chaucer.htm
This again has essays plus further critical works.

ORB: The Online Reference Book for Medieval Studies
http://orb.rhodes.edu/encyclop/culture/lit/Chaucer.html
A guide to online resources, including original essays, primary sources, bibliographies and additional links to Chaucer pages.

Scriptorium
http:/www.wsu.ed:8080/~hanly/chaucer/chaucer-html
Offers the Scriptorium which functions as a Chaucer and medieval literature cyber-net. Has information on medieval concepts such as physiology, allegory, and different kinds of love.

Index

Absolon, 46, 49-51
Alison (*Miller's Tale*), 33, 46, 49-50, 69, 71-2
ambiguity, 9, 39, 40, 69, 71, 72, 74, 79, 91, 94, 98, 105, 107
analogue(s), 42, 43, 44, 45, 47, 53
antifeminism, 55, 76, 80, 90, 105
audience, 36, 37, 43, 44, 45, 47, 48, 49, 58, 59, 95, 99
authoritative/authorise, 22, 23, 26, 34, 39, 90, 91, 98, 103, 104, 106
authority/authorities, 10, 16, 22, 24, 38, 39, 42, 49, 61, 65, 70, 71, 74, 82, 84, 85, 86, 87, 88, 89, 91, 92, 93, 94, 95, 96, 97, 98, 99, 100, 101, 102, 103, 104, 105, 106, 107, 108
authorship/authorial, 14, 32, 91

Canon's Yeoman, the, 24, 40, 55
Canon's Yeoman's Tale, The, 15, 43, 59
Canterbury Tales, The, 9, 14, 15, 16, 17, 18, 20, 23, 28, 29, 30, 39, 41, 42, 47, 52, 62

Cecilia, 45, 47, 62, 63, 65-6, 69, 73-4, 79
Chaucer, Geoffrey (the author), 9, 10, 11-15, 16, 17, 23, 26, 29, 31, 32, 33, 38, 40, 41, 42, 43, 44-9, 50-2, 53, 54, 55, 56, 58, 59, 60, 61, 62, 64, 69, 70, 71, 72, 73, 74, 76, 77, 78, 79, 80-1, 82, 83, 84, 85, 86, 87, 88, 89, 91, 92, 93, 94, 95, 98, 100, 104, 105, 106, 107, 108
Chaucer-the-pilgrim, 16, 17, 18, 26-32, 34, 38, 39, 40, 42, 55
Christ, 30, 36, 57, 65, 67, 69, 78, 86, 88, 89, 95, 96, 103
Christian, 35, 37, 44, 62, 65, 86, 88, 89, 92, 100, 103
chronicler, *see* translator
Church, the, 20, 22, 35, 46, 58, 61, 77, 85, 89, 91-2, 94-5
clerics/clerical teaching, 37, 61-2, 76-7, 84-92, 95-7, 103, 104, 105, 106
Clerk, the, 18, 22, 34-9, 66, 69, 80, 81
Clerk's Tale, The, 23, 34-9, 59, 69, 74, 80-1
closure, 71, 79, 81, 82, 94
comedy/comic, *see* humour, 22, 23, 39, 46, 50, 51, 53,

73, 76, 80, 104
Cook, the, 18, 31-2, 40
courtly love/ courtly lover, 47, 49, 50, 52, 56
critique/criticise, 52, 53, 58, 69, 74, 77, 97, 104, 105
Custance, 43-5, 63, 64, 65, 66-9, 77-8, 79, 82

dramatic frame, 16, 19, 20, 21, 26, 27, 30, 39-40, 44, 48, 87, 101
dream visions, 42, 47, 60

exemplum/example/exemplary, 38, 63, 64, 68, 69, 78, 80, 82, 96, 97, 106
experience/everyday, *see* knowledge, 9, 10, 22, 50, 51, 84, 87, 89, 93, 94, 96, 97, 98, 100, 104, 105, 106, 107

fable, 9, 22, 24, 42, 56
fabliaux, 9, 42, 46, 49, 50, 52
fairy tale/story, 9, 43, 52, 59, 68, 70, 79
folk tales/folk lore, 42, 43, 44
Franklin's Tale, The, 90, 92
Friar, the, 19, 26, 85, 101, 102

General Prologue, 15, 16, 17, 18, 20, 21, 33, 55, 69
generic, 42, 43, 44, 45, 47, 48, 49, 50, 59, 66
genre, see story, 42-52, 56, 59, 66, 106
Griselda, 34-7, 63, 64-5, 66, 69, 74, 79, 80, 81

Harry Bailly/the Host, 16-24, 26, 28, 30, 32, 39, 40, 48, 51, 55, 56, 81
holy/holiness, 36, 45, 62, 63, 64, 68-9, 73
humour/humorous, 20, 22, 24, 30, 50, 51, 73, 79, 98, 105

ideals/idealised/idealising, 34, 35, 38, 50, 51, 61-70, 71-83, 84, 85, 92, 94, 95, 96, 97, 100, 104, 106, 107, 108
institution/institutionalised/ institutionalising, 10, 58, 61, 84, 85, 87, 91, 95, 105, 106
interjection/intervention/ interruption, 9, 18, 20, 36, 37, 39, 51, 66, 67, 77
interpretation/reading, 16, 17, 24, 26, 29, 31-2, 33, 38, 39, 43, 44, 45, 56, 58, 59, 67, 81, 95-7, 98, 103, 106, 107
intertextuality, 31, 40, 58

Januarie, 73, 86-7, 97, 98
John the Carpenter, 50-1, 87-9, 91
juxtaposition/contrast, 49, 71, 72, 106, 107

Knight, the, 33, 34, 48
Knight's Tale, The, 15, 50, 51, 52, 54
knowledge and learning, 56, 84-91, 95-8, 100, 106

Index

lesson, 36, 37, 69, 80, 81, 97
love, *see also* marriage, 47, 49, 50, 51, 55, 77, 80, 86

Man of Law, the, 29, 43, 55, 66-9, 77-8
Man of Law's Tale, The, 18, 23, 29, 40, 43-5, 53, 55, 59, 66-9, 73, 77-8, 82
marriage, 34, 43, 44, 46, 47, 55, 56, 61-2, 63, 73, 75, 77, 79, 80, 84-7, 90, 93, 95
material/tangible, 58, 84, 91-2, 97, 98, 100, 102, 104, 106, 107
May, 72, 73, 77, 82, 97, 98
meek/meekness, 35, 36, 38, 61, 62, 64, 65, 69, 74, 75
Melibee, 32, 43
Merchant, the, 23, 87
Merchant's Tale, The, 23, 40, 72-3, 77, 82, 86-7, 97-8
Miller, the, 24, 26, 31, 34, 46, 54
Miller's Tale, The, 31, 33, 48, 49-52, 54, 69, 71-2, 77, 87-9, 91
Monk, the, 24, 48, 55
Monk's Tale, The, 48-9
moral/morality, 17, 22, 29, 30, 35, 37, 48, 50, 51, 52, 56, 57, 58, 80, 101
multi-layered, 24, 56
multiplication/multiplicity/multiple, 9, 34, 39, 40, 42, 43, 45, 56, 58, 59, 69, 93, 105, 107

narrative/narration, *see also* genre/story, 17, 24, 26, 27, 29, 30-1, 34, 35-7, 39, 41, 42, 45, 54, 55, 59, 61, 66-7, 68, 69, 71, 73, 77, 78, 105, 106
narrator, 28, 33, 37, 39, 41, 42, 43, 44, 45, 54, 55, 56, 61, 63, 66-7, 68, 69, 73, 78, 87, 101
Nicholas, 46, 49-51, 72, 87-9
Nun's Priest, the, 24, 48, 55-6
Nun's Priest's Tale, The, 15, 23, 52, 55-6, 92, 107

open/openness/open-ended, 38, 39, 56, 59, 69, 72, 78, 80, 81, 91, 98, 105, 107

Pardoner, the, 20-3, 26, 33, 40, 57-9, 85, 91-2, 94-5, 98, 99-100
Pardoner's Prologue, The, 91-2, 94-5
Pardoner's Tale, The, 21, 56-9, 99-100
Parson, the, 19, 43, 54, 55, 61-2, 64, 84-6
Parson's Tale, The, 15, 52, 61-2, 87
physical/physicality (the body), 46, 49, 50, 51, 61-2, 75, 80, 100, 101, 102, 104, 105
Physician's Tale, The, 20, 69
Prioress, the, 18, 33, 70

quarrel, quarrelling, 19-20, 31

Index

quiting, 19-20, 24, 31, 40

Reeve, the, 24, 31, 32, 34, 46, 54
Reeve's Tale, The, 31, 46, 50
religion/religious values, 36, 44, 61, 93, 94-5, 103
Retracciouns, 18 29
romance, 9, 42, 43, 44, 47, 60

saints/saintliness/sanctity, 35, 37, 46, 63, 64, 65, 66, 72, 73, 79, 83
saints' lives, 9, 42, 47, 106
Second Nun, the, 45, 55, 85
Second Nun's Tale, The, 40, 45-6, 47-8, 62, 65
sermon, 9, 22, 42, 43, 54, 57, 58, 92, 94, 99
sex, 50, 51, 53, 73, 75, 77-80, 84
Shipman's Tale, The, 20, 55
silence, 38, 61, 62, 64, 65, 69, 70, 71, 73, 78, 81, 88, 90, 100
speaker, 16, 17, 18, 26-7, 29-30, 34, 54, 55, 59, 71
spiritual, 50, 58, 100, 101, 102, 103, 104, 105, 108
story telling, 16-17, 18, 24, 40, 44, 45, 47, 49, 56, 106
story/stories, 19, 24, 29, 31, 41, 42, 43, 47, 50, 52, 55, 56, 57, 58, 66, 67, 80, 90, 102
subversive/subversion, 10, 71, 74, 76, 81, 94, 101-05, 108
Summoner, the, 19, 26, 33, 101, 102, 103, 101-05
*Summoner's Tale, The,*101-05

tales(s), 20, 22, 23, 24, 27, 28, 29, 31, 32, 34, 38, 39, 41, 42, 43, 44, 47, 48, 49, 50, 51, 52, 53, 54, 55, 56, 57, 58, 59, 60, 62, 63, 65, 67, 68, 69, 70, 71, 73, 74, 77, 78, 79, 80, 81, 82, 83, 84, 85, 86, 87, 90, 91, 92, 97, 98, 99, 101, 102, 104, 105, 106, 107, 108
teller, 41, 54, 58, 59, 60
terminology/language, 11-12, 20, 21, 35, 45, 46, 49-50, 52, 57, 66-7, 68-9, 72, 94-5, 99-100
The Tale of Melibee, 22, 28, 29, 92, 107
The Tale of Sir Thopas, 20, 22, 28, 30
translator, *see* chronicler, 26, 27, 30, 31, 39, 42

undercut, 16, 22, 71, 72, 73, 82, 92

virtue/virtuous, 35, 43, 46, 61, 62, 63, 65, 66, 67, 69
voice, *see also* narrator/speaker, 9, 16-17, 18, 26, 29, 30, 31, 32, 33, 34, 38, 39, 40, 42, 43, 44, 54, 55, 58, 59, 66, 68, 71, 73, 76, 100, 105, 106

Walter, 34-6, 63, 74

Wife of Bath, the (Alison), 19, 33, 38, 40, 55, 58, 59, 65, 69, 73, 74-6, 79-80, 81, 85, 89-91, 95-7, 105-6
Wife of Bath's Prologue, The, 19, 27, 55, 59, 75-7, 79-80, 90-1, 95-7, 106
Wife of Bath's Tale, The, 19, 52, 59, 106
women, 22-3, 37-8, 39, 43, 55, 61-70, 72-83, 86, 87, 90-1, 93, 97-8, 106
writing/written, 9, 29, 42, 45, 47, 52, 56, 81, 82, 83, 84, 90-1, 93, 98, 103, 104, 105, 107

Other Studymates titles

Cultural Studies
A student's guide to culture, politics and society
Philip Bounds PhD

Most students of the Humanities/Social Sciences have the opportunity to take courses in Cultural Studies, either as an independent subject or as part of a syllabus in other areas such as Art History, Literary Studies and Sociology. This book meets the need for a concise introduction to Cultural Studies as it has taken shape in Britain. It is unique among introductory texts in combining themes, key writers and historical background to provide an excellent overview for students. Philip Bounds is a Lecturer in Cultural, Media and Film Studies.
Studymates paperback 1 84025 125 5

The European Reformation
A student's guide to the key ideas and the events they shaped
Andrew Chibi PhD

Lecturers often lack the time to present this important subject as fully as students need. Students tend to be either blitzed with information unfamiliar to them or presented with only the barest details, and expected to fill in the gaps themselves. Resource collections are limited and students often left out in the cold. Specially written by an experienced university history lecturer, this new **Studymate** presents the key facts of the European Reformation in a straightforward and student-friendly fashion to help the student understand very clearly the key reformers and their basic reforming principles. Complete with quick summaries and mini-tutorials, this book will meet the needs of lecturers and students alike.
Studymates paperback 1 84025 130 1

GCSE English
The student-friendly way to winning higher grades in GCSE English
Michael Owen BA(Hons)

Universities and employers everywhere want applicants with good reading, writing, speaking and listening skills. That is why English is such an important GCSE to do well in. This Studymate starts with coursework and finishes with the exam; it gives lots of helpful tips and examples, showing how to improve your performance, gain better marks and achieve a higher grade. This book is specially for you if you are taking your GCSE in England, Wales or Northern Ireland; the syllabuses of all six examination boards are followed here. Michael Owen is an experienced teacher and GCSE English examiner. He is Head of English in a secondary school, and helps to train other English teachers. Most important, his methods really work. The number of his own students passing GCSE English with grades A* to C has almost doubled in recent years.
Studymates paperback 1 84025 104 2

Other Studymates titles

Hitler & Nazi Germany
A concise study and revision guide for coursework and exams
Robert Johnson PhD, with a Foreword by Professor Jeremy Black

Are you studying twentieth century German history? Can you give a convincing account in discussion or essays of Hitler and Nazi Germany? How will you gather your evidence, and weigh the historical arguments? That's where this Studymate comes in. It will give you rapid access to the central themes, events and background, and to the key issues raised by this challenging episode of European history. You can use it as a study or revision guide, or as an effective starting point for your course. It is designed to help you build your skills as a history student, and improve your performance in essays, seminars, classes, and exams.
Studymates paperback 1 84025 165 4

Macroeconomics
A student's guide to theory and concepts
Professor R C Brewer & Jerry Mushin BSc(Hons)

Are you studying economics at college or university? Then this book is for you. It will help you to get to grips with this important subject, which so many students find difficult. Written in plain English, it focuses on the key concepts and principles of macroeconomics. Its style is clear and concise, yet rigorous. The use of advanced mathematics is avoided. In this way you should be able to learn and revise more effectively, and tackle your coursework and examinations with much greater confidence. Robert Brewer is a widely published author and examiner in Economics in the UK. Jerry Mushin graduated from the University of London and is now Senior Lecturer in Economics at the Victoria University of Wellington, New Zealand.
Studymates paperback 1 84025 142 5

Practical Drama & Theatre Arts
A skills-based introduction for students, performers and technicians
David Chadderton BA(Hons)

Concise, practical and readable, here is a really great introduction to the theory and practice of creating theatre. Written by an experienced teacher and practitioner, it is an ideal starting point for students, at school, college or in the wider community, wanting to gain the skills to succeed as performers, writers, directors, designers or technicians. Use this book to gain the ideas, experience and qualifications you need to succeed. David Chadderton is based at the Mainstream Dance & Theatre Arts Centre in Manchester. He teaches open drama workshops and diploma classes, produces new courses, provides workshops, arranges liaison for schools, and is active on many drama and theatre projects. He also holds the City & Guilds Certificate in Further & Adult Education.
Studymates paperback 1 84025 109 3

Other Studymates titles

Speaking Better French
Achieving fluency with everyday expressions
Monique Jackman

As with English, the French language includes lots of words and phrases which seem to mean the same thing, but which actually have a different meaning. For example, 'to know' can be *connaitre* (to know someone) or *savoir* (to know something). The student who learns such distinctions will soon progress to fluency. Intended for students with some basic knowledge of French this book will rapidly improve their effectiveness and fluency, by learning and practising these different forms in every situations. A qualified further education teacher, Monique Jackman was born in Marseilles but has lived and taught French in adult education in the UK for almost 20 years.
Studymates paperback 1 84025 136 0

Speaking English
Handling everyday situations with confidence
Dorothy Massey BA(Eng) DipEd CertTESLA

Students living in Britain, or other English-speaking countries, need effective spoken English to enable them to handle everyday situations with confidence. This new handbook will provide students with all the vocabulary and grammar necessary to deal realistically and successfully with both formal and informal encounters, from giving personal and family information, to dealing with health matters, education, the workplace and other vital topics. This very practical book includes a glossary, useful addresses section, web sites for students of English, further reading section, and index. Above all this new Studymate reflects a diverse, changing and multicultural British society.
Studymates paperback 1 84025 114 X

Studying Literature
A student's guide to reading and understanding literary works
Derek Soles PhD

A-level and first year university literature students will welcome this handy introduction to studying literature. Straightforward and very concise, it defines and describes the components of the major literary genres and of literary theory. It covers: the conventions of literary genres, sequencing of events, characters, the narrator, the setting, the message, metaphor, imagery and symbolism, the tone of writing, and the relevance of the author's life and reader's own perspective. It explains traditional analytic methods, and brings you right up to date with more theoretical approaches, too. Step-by-step it gives student-friendly explanations which will boost your performance in coursework and exams. Derek Soles BA(Hons) MA PhD teaches English literature at both undergraduate and postgraduate levels, and is author of *Lessons in Essay Writing* (Prentice Hall).
Studymates paperback 1 84025 131 X

Other Studymates titles

Studying Poetry
Key skills and concepts for literature students
Richard Cochrane BA(Hons) PhD

Do you need to write about poetry? Do you find it frustrating? Is it difficult to find much to say? In this book you will discover the key to understanding poetry, and the secrets which will raise your grades in coursework and exams. This book shows you how poetry works and how to make sense of it. It's full of practical explanations of advanced ideas which will radically improve your performance as a student. It covers traditional analytic methods, and brings you right up to date with more theoretical approaches, too. The author takes you through all the main elements of poetry, fitting them into a step-by-step approach which you can use in any situation. Quickly accessible, packed with key examples, and written in a friendly down-to-earth style, this book will equip you with all the skills you need. Richard Cochrane gained a first class honours degree in English from Cardiff University, where he went on to gain his doctorate and become an Academic Tutor in English Literature and Philosophy.
Studymates paperback 1 84025 146 8

Studying History
A practical guide to successful essay-writing, seminars, assignments and exams
Robert Johnson BA(Hons) PhD

Are you taking a history course at college or university? Do you know what the examiners are really looking for today? Can you gather evidence effectively, weigh the historical arguments, and present a convincing case in person or on paper? That's where this Studymate comes in. It has been specially designed to help you build your critical and analytical skills as a history student. Follow the step-by-step advice in this practical guide, and discover how you can radically improve your performance in essays, seminars, projects, classes, and examinations. The author, Robert Johnson is a graduate of Warwick and Exeter Universities. He is a successful history lecturer, tutor and course manager, and an active member of the Historical Association. He is also author of *Hitler & Nazi Germany* in the Studymates series.
Studymates paperback 1 84025 171 9

Understanding Maths
A practical survival guide to basic maths for students in further and higher education
Graham Lawlor MA

Are you enrolled on an arts or social sciences course in further and higher education, or a training course for work? Do you find it hard to cope with fractions, percentages, averages, decimals, angles, area, volume, or other number and data-related work? Then this is definitely the book for you. Written by an experienced and sympathetic maths teacher, it will help you master all these important skills. Whether you are just starting at college or university, or a mature student, it explains in easy steps everything you need for successful number and data handling.
Studymates paperback 1 84025 124 7